Hezekiah Butterworth

Cruising in the Indian seas

Or, Zigzag Journeys in the Antipodes

Hezekiah Butterworth

Cruising in the Indian seas
Or, Zigzag Journeys in the Antipodes

ISBN/EAN: 9783744757737

Printed in Europe, USA, Canada, Australia, Japan

Cover: Foto ©Andreas Hilbeck / pixelio.de

More available books at **www.hansebooks.com**

"A DOG DRIVING HOME A HORSE FOR HELP FOR HIS DRUNKEN MASTER WHO HAD FALLEN FROM THE CARRIAGE." — Page 111.

OR,

ZIGZAG JOURNEYS IN THE ANTIPODES.

BY

HEZEKIAH BUTTERWORTH.

FULLY ILLUSTRATED.

New York:
GEORGE SULLY,
PUBLISHER.

University Press:
JOHN WILSON AND SON, CAMBRIDGE, U.S.A.

PREFACE.

HIS tenth volume of the "ZIGZAG" series of books has a double purpose: (1) To make young people better acquainted with Siam and the islands of the Indian Ocean, and so to aid the teacher in his work; and (2) to illustrate the fact that kindness to harmless and tamable animals, as exemplified in Buddhist countries, adds to the general happiness of mankind.

In preparing the "ZIGZAG" series of books, I have had many helps from experienced travellers; and in this one I am indebted to Mrs. A. H. LEONOWENS, author of "The English Governess at the Siamese Court," who was once employed as a governess in the royal court of Siam, for a large part of the matter in the ninth chapter, and to Dr. C. A. STEPHENS for the plan and a part of the work in the chapter on Sumatra. These chapters, in part, originally appeared in the "Youth's Companion," as also the story of the Siamese twins. I have, moreover, received helps from American missionaries in Siam and Burmah.

The "ZIGZAG" books, which are stories of places, are written with the aim of interesting the young in what is at once entertaining and educational. It is hoped that they may lead the young readers to form a taste for the better books of geography, history, legend, and song, that treat the several subjects for more mature minds.

The author feels grateful to the public, and especially to parents and teachers, for the kind and liberal way in which each new volume has been received.

H. BUTTERWORTH.

28 WORCESTER STREET,
   BOSTON, MASS.

CONTENTS.

Chapter		Page
I.	A Telegrapher in a White Mountain Hotel.	15
II.	Finding the Antipodes of the West, and the Christmas of Columbus in the New World	28
III.	Cousin Ivory, and a Letter from Siam	44
IV.	A City ruled by an Elephant.	55
V.	Ayuthia, the Terrestrial Paradise	71
VI.	The most wonderful Ruins of Asia	80
VII.	The Story of the Leper King.	88
VIII.	Ivory in Florida	95
IX.	Ivory's strange Stories	115
X.	Java. — The Story of the Flying Dutchwoman	148
XI.	Bangkok	179
XII.	The Siamese Twins	196
XIII.	The Adventures of a Lineman in Sumatra.	207
XIV.	Java, and the Flying Dutchman	229
XV.	Bangkok again	250
XVI.	The Fate of the Seven Merchants who believed Lies	283
XVII.	The Cremation of a King	309
XVIII.	Ivory's Death	316

ILLUSTRATIONS.

	PAGE
"A dog driving home a horse for help for his drunken master who had fallen from the carriage" . . . . *Frontispiece*	
"It was a lonely house, deserted by its builders"	16
"I was reported to have pursued him at a wild pace through the woods" . .	19
"I used to shoot at everything, whether it were good to eat or not"	23
"Naples, where he would see the fires of Vesuvius gleaming on the emerald deeps of the summer sea"	29
"The boy-dreamer of Genoa — for it was he — told him his dream" . . .	35
"Land is nigh," he said; "we shall see it in the morning"	38
The Harbor of Havana	41
Drifting up the Meinam in May . . .	45
Map of Siam	47
He "points toward the dazzling light and says, 'Bangkok'"	49
A Patriarch of a Monkey and his Family	51
"The morning will find us in Bangkok"	53
"For, you know, the Buddhists believe that men are reborn according to merit"	56
The Elephants' Kraal	57
"The palace itself is a wonder" . . .	61
Driving Wild Elephants into the Kraal .	64
Royal Audience Hall at Bangkok . .	65
The King as a Boy	69
"The royal city of Ayuthia" . . .	73
Ruins of the Golden Mountain . . .	77
"I enclose a picture"	80
The Leper King	81
"The temple covered an area of ten acres"	83
The Giant Bridge at Angker, restored .	87
"Its domes were like stars, and its pinnacles like jewels"	89
"The King from the Lotus Land started on a long journey"	93
"By the gate of the palace he sat, the Leper King"	94
The White Heron	97
Birds on the Indian River	101
The River Ouse goes dimpling by . .	105
Cowper's House at Olney	109
"The orioles are weavers"	112
"Swallows that frequent the surf-beaten caves"	113
The Astrologer from Siam	118
"Moonsee can burn water"	119
"We had gone out into the court to enjoy the cooler air"	125
"The pious fakir rolled down his back"	129
"A very wise king he must have been"	132
"The rachassee and the elephant are usually placed on the outside of the temples"	133
"Its fond mother first brought it into the sitting-room in her mouth" . .	137
"Her eyes were filled with reproach" .	141
"She's brought it home, basket and all"	143
"A negro boy violently kicked him" .	145
A Javan Basket-Merchant	149
"She did not look as though she could fly"	152
The Java Coffee-Market	153

ILLUSTRATIONS.

	PAGE
"The fishermen said she had wings"	155
The great Buddhist Temple of Java	157
"Here the local sportsmen sought them"	161
"He had turned around with wild eyes, and fled"	165
A Bamboo Bridge	169
A Roadside in Java	173
"People seemed to live on the water"	177
"Within these walls reside none but women"	181
Siamese Dramatic Artists	185
The Ceremonial of Shaving the Hair	189
"He shot an arrow into the air"	193
Ladies dining in the Inner City	197
The Siamese Twins	199
Javan Women dancing	201
A Javan Home	205
"Down the valley of the River Busar"	209
A little Suspension Bridge of Bamboo	212
A Scene in Sumatra	213
"Others were breaking down or wrenching out the posts"	217
"So he sent for his lords and attendants, and they all set off together"	220
"On he rode as fast as before, with the tree in his hand"	223
An Avenue in Batavia	227
Chinese devoured by Man-eating Tigers	231
"And yet the mice do not love the cat"	234
"Vessels went out of Amsterdam empty"	236
"A strange form appeared on the deck"	237
"He would have to sail away again"	241
"He is doomed to sail forever"	243
"Like to a vision, seen in days long by-gone"	247
"Many millions more for sport"	251
An Idolatrous Habit	253
"They met a forlorn donkey"	255
"Now, the building was not a temple, but the palace of a Rakshas"	257
Idol of the God of Wisdom	260
"The same eternal figure of Buddha"	261
"Both girls were laughing and shrieking, and making merry over their work"	263
"We walked by the canal"	267
"In the fall the river overflows its banks"	272
"The driver sat on the head of the elephant"	273
A Pagoda in the Laos	275
A Marriage Ceremony in Java	279
On a Bamboo Raft	285
Rafting Teak-Wood	289
A Village in the Upper Laos	293
The City of Xieng Maï, in the Upper Laos	297
"He seized the man and was about to devour him"	301
"The elephant begged for a week's delay"	305
A Break-Neck Ride	311
Ivory's Tomb at Bangkok	317

CRUISING IN THE INDIAN SEAS.

ZIGZAG JOURNEYS IN THE ANTIPODES.

CHAPTER I.

A TELEGRAPHER IN A WHITE MOUNTAIN HOTEL.

HAD never thought much about the sacredness of all life, animal as well as human, until I met my cousin Ivory, from Siam. I was employed as tutor in the family of one of the great White Mountain hotel-keepers in the summer, and I held the same position in a Florida hotel in winter, both houses having the same proprietor.

I was fond of the gun, and I had never been taught that there was anything more wrong or cruel in killing a bird or an animal without a purpose, than in cutting down a shrub or a plant. None of my teachers had ever said anything to me upon the subject. I had never heard so much as a suggestion concerning it in the church or the Sunday-school. I had read something about the subject in Thoreau's "Walden;" that was all.

I had been sent to school in an old red school-house among the Granite Hills, in the town where the hotel was situated. The school-house had a terrible tradition. It was a lonely house, deserted by its builders, and adapted to its altered use by an economical school-committee where land was cheap. The house, one fall, obtained the dark reputation of being haunted. The children's lunches often disappeared in a way that was unaccountable. In early spring the story had been revived, as strange noises were heard under the building. One day, at recess, one of the pupils discovered a large hole under the foundations of the building; and through the opening appeared a long, brown nose, almost as large as that of a horse. What could it be? The more

"IT WAS A LONELY HOUSE, DESERTED BY ITS BUILDERS."

adventurous boys threw sticks and stones at the mysterious nose, when there emerged from the hole a long head and a great shaggy body.

"A bear!" shouted all; and there was a flying of feet inside of the doors.

The faces of the teacher and of all the boys and girls filled the windows, and a large bear was seen swaying to and fro from the house toward a long strip of pine that led to the hills. Had the bear been under the house all winter? Was another there? Would he return?

Not only the school, but the whole neighborhood had been thrown into a great state of excitement by this queer event. The boys organized an Anti-Bear Club, and made me their leader. I felt very heroic over the honor. To be the Chief of the Anti-Bear Club, in this time of excitement, was no common trust. I felt its importance duly; and to prepare myself for some future great encounter with Bruin, I began to wage war on innocent rabbits and otters, and the whole animal kingdom. We armed ourselves with bows and arrows, and began to practise at a mark which we seldom failed not to hit; and if the mark had been the bear, the arrows would not have given him so much as a scratch. People began to carry guns in their wagons when they were to pass through lonely roads, and especially when they went to mill, as the mill was on a secluded waterfall far from the main way. I had been accustomed to go to mill on horseback, sitting upon the grist like a saddle.

"Manton," said my father to me one day, "we are out of meal."

"I will go to mill," said I, "but I must have the gun."

"The gun! Pooh! What for?"

"Why, you know, — the bear."

"But you don't need the gun on horseback. The horse would save you, if you should see the bear."

"Yes; but I could not kill the bear."

"True, Manton, true, — well, take the gun."

The horse was a young one and quite nervous; but he had carried grists to the mill several times in safety, shying at times at a stump or a noise in the bushes by the wayside. I never felt more proud in my life than when I mounted the horse on the bag, and father handed me the gun. Had I not seen a like picture in the "Trappers' Tales"?

I turned the gun in an inverse angle under my left arm, for it was in this picturesque way that I fancied I had seen it carried by some pictured Mexican on the plains. In making this curious manœuvre I chanced to hit the pony, and the latter began to wheel round and round. At each circle the gun would strike him again, and he seemed to become very suspicious that the gun was not a proper thing to carry. But after much excitement he came under control, and I started toward the mill.

It was a fragrant morning in spring; the snow was melting on the mountains, and there were cascades everywhere. The bluebirds had come, and the red-headed woodpeckers were tapping the trees. The sun was all radiance, glimmering amid the hemlocks; and I, the Chief of the Anti-Bear Club, rode on, longing for an adventure that would justify my title to that honor. But no bear appeared. I began to hear the mill-wheel turning in the distance, and felt a shadow of disappointment at not having met the bear.

At this unheroic juncture a little rabbit chanced to run into the road. I whistled. He pricked up his ears and stopped. I was full of the impulse to use the gun, and turned the latter suddenly and fired. The earth seemed to collapse with the report of the gun. I know not how it all came about so suddenly. I recall finding myself on the ground in a heap of shelled corn, of seeing a rabbit's tail disappearing in the bushes, and the very much longer tail of a wild pony forming a curve over a side hill. I was greatly shocked and amazed. Just then an animal moved in some bushes by the roadside. It might have been the bear. I never knew. If I could not kill the bear, I was resolved that the Chief of the Anti-Bear Club at least should not be devoured by the bear; and leaving the gun in the road, I flew toward the mill.

It was a terrible tale of adventure that I had to tell the miller. The latter told it to the farmers as they came with their grists. The excitement grew. I recovered my gun and returned home on foot.

"I WAS REPORTED TO HAVE PURSUED HIM AT A WILD PACE THROUGH THE WOODS."

My mother received me gratefully, and said it was a "narrer escape." The pony had returned, but he would not allow me to approach him for weeks. As for father, he merely said: "Well, Manton, ye made a rather *scatterin'* voyage."

The bear story was told at the great hotel when the summer season opened, and had a most ridiculous ending. The old women and servants were often heard cautioning the children of the hotel-boarders not to go far from the grounds nor into the woods, lest they should meet with the dreadful bear and some Little Red Riding-Hood catastrophe should follow. The women of the hotel were very cautious of long excursions, and avoided the beautiful byways of the country. Bruin had become a bugbear indeed, and I was reported to have pursued him at a wild pace through the woods to his lair.

There was a little girl boarder called Flossie. I never knew what her other name was. Her mother was rich and pretentious; a person of newly acquired wealth, I think, as most showy people are. She affected great fear of the perils of country life, and had a great horror that Flossie might be devoured by the bear. The bear would have had a hard time to devour Flossie, with her doll dresses, ribbons, enormous hat, and ornaments. But her mother, many times a day, would look up from her novel to say, "Don't go far, Flossie, on account of the bear."

The bear story grew. All bear stories are apt to grow. A hotel is a good place for a story to grow; boarders of easy means are apt to have very poetic imaginations.

One day I heard Flossie's mother say, "Don't run away, Flossie; remember those little school-children who were *eaten* up by the bear."

"Where were they eaten up by the bear, mother?"

"Oh, I don't know! Don't bother me; the *Bible* tells all about it."

This was an evolution of the local story, indeed. But one day Flossie "runned away," as she called her escapade. It was one morning, toward noon, that a doll-like little figure was seen flying down the near hill, evidently in great terror. Her hat, which was as big as a parasol, was floating behind her on the wind; her ribbons streamed like flags, and her white dress like a wee yacht under full sail. Her mother saw her coming in this alarmed condition, dropped her novel, and like one of her novel's probable heroes or heroines, cried, "My child, my child!" Flossie presently fell down in a little muslin heap on the veranda of the hotel. Her mother picked her up, drew her to her breast, and gasped, "What is it, Flossie?" Flossie sobbed. At last, when somewhat quieted, Flossie ventured to look up into her mother's face.

"What is it, Flossie?"

"I — saw — the — horrid — bear."

"Oh, Flossie! I will not stay here a day longer."

The mother put her adventurous little one down gently, and hurried into the parlor to spread the fearful news. Several guests agreed with the indignant mother that the place was unsafe for women and children, and that they ought to make a change.

Flossie became a heroine. That evening the hotel proprietor, alarmed at the evil reputation which had befallen his house, came into the parlor where the women and the new Little Red Riding-Hood were.

"I think it is a shame to keep a hotel in such a place," said Flossie's mother; and a rich old lady, in a high cap and a stiff satin dress, said plainly, with great dignity and a wave of a feather-fan, —

"And I think so too. A man ought to be prosecuted."

"I think there is some mistake," said the proprietor. "How did the bear look, Flossie?"

"Black, — it was a black bear."

"There!" said Flossie's mother; "could anything be more convincing than that?"

"But how did you know it was a bear? Did you ever see a bear?"

"Yes; I'se seen 'em in the picture-books."

"I USED TO SHOOT AT EVERYTHING, WHETHER IT WERE GOOD TO EAT OR NOT."

"It might have been a black dog."

"No, it was n't, — I *know* it was a bear."

"How, Flossie?"

"He *said* so hisself."

There was an awful silence. The old woman dropped her feather-fan. Had the age of Æsop returned again?

"What did he say, Flossie?"

"He just said, *Ba-a*."

If ever a parlor full of women turned into statues, it was at this dramatic disclosure. The proprietor laid back his head to take breath, and then such an explosion of laughter as followed I have seldom heard. Flossie's mother rose, and said with an injured air, —

"It is time for you to go to bed, Flossie;" and in this opinion there seemed to be a unanimous agreement. I never heard much fear of the bear expressed anywhere, after this episode was made public and became a village story.

But my boyish experience, as the Chief of the Anti-Bear Club, gave me an education in cruelty that I to-day look back upon with horror, and I wonder how I, who have naturally a kind heart, could have done some acts which I did without any disturbance of conscience. I used to shoot at everything, whether it were good to eat or not, or harmful or not; and there is nothing that flies or walks which is really harmful, or not a help to the largest interest of mankind.

I recall breaking the wing of a mother robin while the latter was sitting upon her young brood, and that the act *did* give me a twinge of conscience. I shot at her with an arrow. She dropped from her nest with a broken wing, ran into some briers, and I caught her. I put her in a cage, and she got away twice; and as she could not fly, she tried to hop back to her nest and young. A feeling of pity filled my heart, as I saw this instinct. She and her brood died in a few days. I have to-day no words to express my detestation of such an act. What a brute I was, to deprive this innocent bird of the orchards, the sunshine, her nest, her young, and all that God and Nature had fitted her to enjoy!

Was I to blame? Yes; but there were other conditions of social life to blame. My parents were to blame; my teachers were to blame; the papers and books that I read were to blame; and the dead social conscience was to blame, and all the influences that were indifferent to the sacredness of animal life.

My cousin Ivory? His father was a missionary in Siam. Ivory had come to this country when a boy, and studied two years at the Massachusetts Institute of Technology at Boston, had returned to the Antipodes, and been employed as a lineman in Sumatra. I had met him often when he was in America, had come to like him more than others, and a warm attachment had been formed between us.

Sumatra is a land of strange animals, and I read with an eager interest Ivory's letters, that were full of stories of adventures among animals which opposed his work on the telegraph lines. But these letters had a very different spirit from those of American boys in the East or West. There was a kindliness in them that I could not understand. We came to speak of Ivory as our cousin in the Antipodes.

After several years' work in telegraph building in Sumatra, Java, and Siam, I received a letter from him which greatly pleased me. I had become a tutor then.

"Who do you suppose is about to visit me?" I asked of my pupils one day.

"Your friend Harry from the Plains," said one, with expectation.

"No; my cousin Ivory from the Antipodes."

"What are the Antipodes?" asked all.

"The people whose feet are turned toward ours."

"Does your cousin Ivory walk with his feet turned toward ours?" asked a lad.

"Yes."

"With his head hanging down over nothing? I should think that he would fall off."

"Where would he go to?" asked another.

I promised my pupils that our next studies in geography should be the Antipodes; and at our next session I related to them the following story.

CHAPTER II.

FINDING THE ANTIPODES OF THE WEST, AND THE CHRISTMAS OF COLUMBUS IN THE NEW WORLD.

ABOUT four hundred and thirty years ago, an Italian boy was sitting upon one of the old quays of Genoa, gazing upon the evening star. He had recently returned from the University at Pavia, and knew something of astronomy. He was not like other boys, although he knew not why at the time,—he afterward said that a Divine calling to perform some unknown mission had impressed itself upon him in his boyhood, and that it was this which gave his mind and feet no rest in his early years.

The star seemed hanging in the liquid air. How did it come there? What held it? Was it a sphere? What if this earth itself were a star, hanging like a sphere in space? If so, half of this earth-star was unknown. He dreamed, perhaps, that he was upon another planet, and found it looked out into the heavens for the earth. Night came: the celestial scenery began to appear; the great planets shone like astrals. Then in his dream appeared the earth. It was a little star. What if he could sail away into the unknown regions of the ocean, and find there an undiscovered hemisphere?

The shadows were falling upon Genoa, and stars like lamps were appearing over the dark walls of the mountains. The city stood white in the gathering gloom; lights twinkled in the cool balconies, and the boats came in from the sea.

The boy sat dreaming. In his studies he had met with a Latin author, Seneca. The works of this author contained a strange prophecy, and in it were the Latin words *Ultima Thule*,—"the last world." The words "Ultima Thule" seemed spoken to his soul. Very early in his life, perhaps at this very hour, they began to haunt him, and make his imagination restless. "Ultima Thule! Ultima Thule!" rang in his ears.

"NAPLES, WHERE HE WOULD SEE THE FIRES OF VESUVIUS GLEAMING ON THE EMERALD DEEPS OF THE SUMMER SEA."

The boy was poor. He must become a sailor, — most poor boys of Genoa became sailors. In a few days he would make his first voyage; it would be to Naples, where he would see the fires of Vesuvius gleaming on the emerald deeps of the summer sea. He had a very religious nature, and he was a lover of church music and the old Latin hymns. There was one hymn that the sailors used to sing; it was a hymn to a star. The Virgin was represented in it as a Star. When the boy first heard this hymn we do not know, but it became the hymn of his soul, — "Ave Maria Stella."

> "Gentle Star of Ocean,
> Portal of the sky!
> Ever Virgin Mother
> Of the Lord Most High!"

There were two stanzas of this old hymn that expressed his aspiration and feeling, —

> "Still, as on we journey,
> Help our weak endeavor,
> Till with Thee and Jesus
> We rejoice forever.
>
> "Through the highest heaven
> To the Almighty Three,
> Father, Son, and Spirit,
> Equal glory be!"

The beautiful night was filled with stars, as the boy turned away from the lonely quay, and made his way through the silent streets to his simple home. The stars seemed all around him like the lamps of a celestial city. What if the earth itself were but one of them? What if the earth were a star?

In 1459 the boy sailed away under the bright banners of John of Anjou, in the expedition of that Duke to gain the crown of Naples. From that day he became a sailor, and lived for years almost constantly upon the Mediterranean. But wherever he went the dream of his boyhood came back, ever with more distinctness. His mind was haunted by his star.

The boy, a young man now, began to hear strange stories of the bold sailors of Henry of Portugal. These Portuguese adventurers were believed to have discovered the Fortunate Islands, the Hesperian Gardens of the Golden Age. They were venturing farther and farther upon the unknown ocean, and were filling Portugal with wonderful stories of what they had found and seen.

It was believed at this time that beyond the known ocean was a sea of monsters, and that this sea was eternally dark, and that they who should venture near it would be devoured by sea dragons or serpents of horrid shapes and gigantic forms. Nothing could be more horrible than this imaginary dark sea.

The Portuguese, however, did not find it. The ocean, wherever they ventured, was calm and beautiful, and lighted with stars. There was no eternal darkness and there were no monsters. But the sky in summer was often fiery, and it came to be believed by many that instead of an ocean of darkness and monsters the sea was bounded by awful gulfs of fire, and that those who dared to go beyond a certain imaginary boundary would never return, — that they would sail into billows of fire, and so be destroyed.

Prince Henry of Portugal had become intensely interested in the navigators' tales. He established a naval college and erected an observatory, and became the patron of adventurous navigators. He, too, began to dream of islands and peopled regions beyond the known limits of the sea. The mariner's compass under his influence came into general use. Ships sailed into the tropics, and were not lost either in darkness or in flames. The African coast became known, and the beautiful Azore Islands.

The boy dreamer heard of these wonderful things. His restless imagination made his feet restless. He must go to Portugal. Not for wealth, not for fame, but because he had dreamed a dream that was greater than had entered other minds, because a Divine influence seemed to inspire him and impel him, he must go. He had seen a star.

He arrived at Lisbon in 1470, a young man, handsome and courtly, but lonely and mysterious. His dream had become his life. He had not been like other boys, and now he was not like other men. But those who came to know him loved him greatly; and among them Dona Felipa, the daughter of an Italian cavalier, one of Prince Henry's navigators, whom he married.

He still loved the stars, and gazed wistfully toward the mysterious sea, and dreamed. The words "Ultima Thule" still haunted him; something awaited him that did not belong to the destiny of other men, — what, he did not know. He loved the Church, and secret communion with God. It was his delight to hide away in the Chapel of All Saints; to go away from the vision of the stars to seek the direction of Him who had created all things and knew the great secrets of all. He studied maps and navigation continually, and listened to all the tales that the sea adventurers told. The conviction settled more and more upon him that a large portion of the earth must be unexplored. What was there? Darkness? Fire? Beautiful lands, islands, and seas?

The far ocean had been found so wonderfully beautiful that people now began to dream that Paradise was there, with seven cities, built by seven lost Bishops whom the Moors had driven to sea.

The dreamer still saw the Evening Star glowing in the west, in the glimmering horizon that seemed to blend with the sea. What was in the west? His soul longed to follow the star, but he was poor. He had a soul to dare the sea, but he was so poor in influence and purse that he could not command a sail.

At this time a great scientific discovery was made, — the astrolabe,[1] by which the sailor was freed from his bondage to the land, as it enabled him to find the land again wherever he might travel the sea.

The dreamer of Genoa now saw his opportunity. He saw in the new invention the sceptre of the sea, the key to the ocean's mysteries.

He went to King John of Portugal. He asked for ships to sail into the west, — to follow the Star. He told the king that he believed that Asia could be reached by sailing west, and that he could discover the island of Cipango, the supposed treasure-island of the far seas, and return from this island to enrich the King and make glorious his reign. The King referred the matter to a learned Council. The Council ridiculed the dream, and the dreamer left the Court with a sad heart.

But the dream haunted the King. Suppose it were true? Crowns enrich themselves by commerce. He resolved to send out a secret expedition of his own, and thus defraud the supposed visionary, should the dream be true.

Among those who listened to the dream was Count Villareal. He was a man of genius and believed the dreamer.

"I am a soldier," he said, "but I am about to prophesy with a spirit and voice that seem to come to me from Heaven: the prince who shall undertake this enterprise will win greater glory and renown than any prince who ever sat upon a throne."

The wife of the Italian dreamer died, and he turned away from Portugal, poor and disheartened, but still rich in his dream. He left behind him debts that he could not pay. He fled secretly, taking with him his only son, Diego (1484). He returned to Genoa, where he had dreamed his childhood dreams. The latter had come to nothing: was the Divine guidance in which he had trusted only a delusion or a fancy? The gates of inspiration had seemed to be open to him; now they seemed closed. But the Star still shone as of old on the far western sea.

The dream came back again. He applied to the Republic of Genoa for ships to explore the western ocean, — to dukes and princes; but all listened to him as to a fairy tale.

The dream grew; it gave him no rest. He resolved to go to Spain and to lay his plan before the sovereigns. It was the golden age of Spain now.

---

[1] Now the quadrant.

The wedded kingdoms of Arragon and Castile, under Ferdinand and Isabella, were triumphing over the Moors. He obtained an audience with the King, who listened to him as to a poet, and, like King John of Portugal, referred the matter to a Council.

The Council met at Salamanca. It consisted of university men of science and of prelates. In the discussion of the theory the prelates thought the conception of a new world contradicted the theology of Saint Augustine and the works of the Latin Fathers, and therefore could not be correct.

"If the world be round," said one of the grave men of science, "then the people on the other side must walk with their feet upward and their heads downward, and that could not be."

"If this theory be true," said another great man, "there can be no heavens over the lower part of the earth."

"As to returning from the voyage," said another, "that would be impossible; for the ship would have to sail *up* the earth, as though it were climbing a mountain. *That* could not be."

How wise these men were! Were there indeed Antipodes? Were there people and countries and seas and islands *under* the earth?

Time passed. Hungry and thirsty, there came one day a traveller to a convent near Palos, leading by the hand a motherless boy. It was high noon, and the traveller stopped in the shade to speak with the prior. The latter asked him who he was; and the boy dreamer of Genoa — for it was he — told him his dream. The prior was a geographer, and listened to the wonderful vision most eagerly. He had influence with the Court, and promised to use it in the interest of an expedition. He did so; but a decision was still delayed.

The dreamer now wandered over Spain in poverty. Though poor from his youth, he had a royal soul, and he dared stand erect in the presence of kings. People now called him a "visionary," and laughed at his rags. The children insulted him in the streets.

"See!" they said, "he is touched in mind. And why is he so forlorn and lonely and meanly dressed?"

Some of the people answered: "He thinks that there are inhabitants *under* the earth."

And others: "He thinks that the earth is a star."

So the uncouth laughed at him, and the better-bred pitied him. They all seemed to pity his little son. But the good prior secured for him the ear of the Queen at last; and she became so much interested in his story that she said that she would be willing to part with her jewels to provide for him ships for such an expedition.

"THE BOY-DREAMER OF GENOA — FOR IT WAS HE — TOLD HIM HIS DREAM."

It is Friday, Aug. 3, 1492. The boy-dreamer of Genoa is now upon the sea with three little vessels, over which float the banner of the Cross and the double crowns of Arragon and Castile. The ships have forced crews, and they move away from Palos amid wondering eyes. Night comes, and from the deck of the caravel the dreamer again sees the Star of the West. An Admiral now, he gazes upon it as when a boy. The same questions haunt him.

"Let us sing," he said to the crew. The evening hymn to the Virgin arose.

> "Gentle Star of Ocean,
> . . . . . .
> Help our weak endeavor,
> Till with Thee and Jesus
> We rejoice forever."

The joy of the Admiral, as he found himself at last upon the sea following the Star beneath the banner of the Cross, was great. His soul must have risen to the gates of Heaven in gratitude, as the crews sang, —

> "Through the highest heaven,
> To the Almighty Three."

The ships went on. They passed the peak of Teneriffe, whose chimney was pouring forth fire, as if warning the sailors of perils to come. But the lateen-sails flew onward. Day by day the sun rose on a placid sea, and night by night the Evening Star burned in the west, and the crews sang the hymn to the Virgin, the "Star of Ocean." Every night they sang this hymn when rose the Evening Star; and the dreamer of Genoa dreamed his old dreams, and "trusted the God who made him, and followed the sea that was silent."

The caravels passed the Canaries, the last known land. The crews shed tears as the last island faded. They had nothing further to trust but the faith in the soul of the Admiral, and he was following a Star.

On, on, amid seas as calm as the sheltered currents of the Guadalquivir, and breezes as soft as "April's in Andalusia," the Polar Star shining nightly through the clear air, and the Evening Star as often appearing amid the roses of the sunset, and the crews as often singing the old Latin hymn, —

> "Gentle Star of Ocean,
> Portal of the sky."

Still on and on. Trade-winds, dazzling showers, and soft calms. A cloud-bank appeared. The crews cried "Land!" and they sang the "Gloria." But the cloud lifted, leaving still the boundless, empty sea. The crews wished to turn back. But the Admiral still gazed on the Star of the Sea; he felt that he was walking the sea by faith, and that faith never faltered.

One morning strange birds came and hovered around the mast. One of them lit upon a spar and sang a song. It was a land bird; its song was a land song,— it had learned it amid the trees. The Admiral's heart beat quickly as he listened. Had the bird not been sent to cheer him? Did not its song say "Hope"? Might not some good angel have inspired the bird? Green herbage came drifting over the sea, and a branch of thorn with a bunch of berries on it,— an olive branch to the Admiral's eye.

"Land is nigh," he said; "we shall see it in the morning."

At sunset the crews sang again, —

"LAND IS NIGH," HE SAID; "WE SHALL SEE IT IN THE MORNING."

"Gentle Star of Ocean, Portal of the sky."

The evening darkened, and the Star appeared. The Star went down; but the mariners, with hearts quivering with emotion, gazed on in the star-lit hours over the dark sea. A far light appeared.

Boom! What signal was that? It was the gun of the "Pinta," the leading ship; and the word that it uttered was "Land!"

The dream of the dreamer of Genoa was now becoming a reality.

Morning came; and with it a new world, — no more a vision, but a very paradise of the sea. The dreamer had solved the mystery of the ocean. He landed, kissed the earth, and gave thanks to God.

Then the little ships went on again, amid the Bahamas, — the palmy Edens of the Western Seas,—amid the singing of birds, the sweet smell of woods, and the odors of flowers. And the Evening Star nightly smiled on those beautiful isles. The long island of Cuba was passed, with its palmy shores and lofty mountains.

They came to Hispaniola. It was near Christmas, and the thought of the Nativity began to fill the soul of the Admiral. Had he not, like the Magi of old, been following a Star by faith; and had not his faith revealed to him the very counsels of Heaven?

On the morning of the 24th of December the Admiral set sail before sunrise, to cross the calm sea to visit a cacique whose acquaintance he had made. The caravel made little progress,—the breeze was so light and the sea so quiet. But it drifted slowly on. Christmas eve was approaching. The sun hung over the isles, the palmy crowns of the seas, as though itself were an island of fire in a sea of dazzling light,—a far gate of heaven between the sea and the sky. The sunset over the glimmering islands passed; then came the afterglow, and with it the pure face of the Star of the Sea.

The Admiral—a man certain of his destiny now, the viceroy of the lands that he had discovered—stood on the light deck of the caravel gazing upon the Star. We may know, from what he afterward wrote, that his thoughts turned toward another star,—the Star of the East. The Divine Presence had long seemed to be with him; and his dream now was of the Nativity, and of those of old who had followed a Star to the cradle of the Lord. When he had gone to Queen Isabella, he had promised to find new lands for the Cross. But a dream which he had thought even more glorious had often passed over his mind. He aspired to accumulate gold, and with it recover the Holy Sepulchre. The islands around him might be stored with mines of gold and treasures. If so, it might be they would furnish him treasure to purchase the Holy Sepulchre. What might not be possible to him to whom Heaven had revealed so much? The Star grew brighter and brighter in the fading afterglow, and he gazed upon it as when a boy at Genoa. It stood out clear and splendid against the darkness at last, and slowly descended toward the sea. He dreamed, as before, wonderful dreams; they were of the Orient now. He did not know that the Star had led him to the cradle lands of the Church, and that here faith would soon lift her golden domes into the air. How strange had been his life! How wonderful it must have seemed this Christmas eve,—the first that ever a Christian had known on these star-lit waters! "God made me," he afterward said, "the messenger of the new heavens and the new earth, and told me where to find them."

Did the crew sing the old Latin hymn that evening? We do not know.

We are told that the hymn was sung every evening during the voyage across the sea. If this Christmas eve it were sung, how wonderfully poetic it must have been! —

> "Gentle Star of Ocean,
> Portal of the sky."

So passed the first Christian Christmas eve in the New World.

That night the ship received an injury by drifting on a sand-bar, and was wrecked in the silent currents of the waveless star-lit sea. The crew and the ship's stores were saved, and the first Christmas day in America was spent by the Viceroy in the saving of the wreck. He built a fortress of the vessel on the shore. The vessel bore the name of the Virgin, — "Santa Maria."

"What shall the castle be called?" asked the men.

"Navidad," said the Viceroy, "La Navidad, — the Fortress of the Nativity. I was wrecked and saved on Christmas day."

He sailed away from the Fortress of the Nativity, leaving a garrison there, to carry the wonderful news to Spain. The learned men would not sneer at him now; the children would not laugh at him in the streets. Such a triumph now awaited him as never any man before received. He would pass in grand processions, in viceregal pomp, over the ways where he had wandered in poverty and loneliness, and would carry a light heart where he had once known only heaviness and pain.

The boy-dreamer of Genoa had seen the Star in the New World. He had found the "Ultima Thule." The prophecy in his young heart had proved true. The earth was a *star*.

And there were Antipodes.

Some months ago I sailed from Tampa, Florida, and arrived near sunset in the harbor of Havana. It was too late to land that night, as no foreign steamer is allowed to land after sunset. So we lay in the beautiful harbor under the guns of Moro Castle, the white city before us, and scores of little boats and noisy boatmen circling around us.

It was Christmas eve. As the sun set, it left a tropic splendor in the sky. The city began to darken under it, and lights to twinkle on the rim of the sea. The towers of the old cathedrals and churches rose stately and grand against the glimmering sky. The Cuban pilot pointed to one of these old churches, as the passengers stood on the deck, and said, "Colon."

"That is the church where *he* is buried," said an American.

All eyes were directed toward it as the light faded. Its antique towers, like two giant arms, uplifted two crosses. The church became slowly lost to

THE HARBOR OF HAVANA.

view in the shadows; but over it hung a light, like the eternal lamp over an altar, which grew more clear as the evening dusk followed the glow in the sky. It was the Star, —

"Gentle Star of Ocean,
Portal of the sky."

The city grew bright with illuminations, and the Christmas bells began to ring. I could but recall the grand words of the prophet of the seas, to whose dust we seemed so near: "God made me the messenger of the new heavens and the new earth, and told me where to find them. Human reason, mathematics, and charts availed me nothing."

There were Antipodes; and the Antipodes of the Antilles are the islands and peninsulas of the far Indian seas.

CHAPTER III.

COUSIN IVORY, AND A LETTER FROM SIAM.

I HAD written to Cousin Ivory about my chieftainship of the Anti-Bear Club, and my various exploits in the destruction of animals and birds, and I supposed that he would be greatly interested in these adventures, and would return to me letters full of like episodes in the wonderful lands and islands of the Antipodes. In those far heathen countries I felt sure that the destruction of animals and birds must be a common experience, and that his adventures must quite outdo those pictured in boys' books relating to our Western Territories, to the Amazons, and to Africa. I was therefore somewhat surprised to receive the following letter, and to note in what a different spirit it was written from my own letter to which it was an answer. The letter was written on a small ship in the river Meinam, on which Ivory had taken passage from Sumatra to Bangkok. Over the date of the letter was a pleasing title to the contents, as though from the letter might be expected a story. This title was —

THE IMITATIVE MONKEYS.

It is a glowing afternoon in May, and I have entered the Meinam, and am within some twenty miles of Bangkok, the great city of temples, palaces, and idols. Above me flies the flag of Siam, a white elephant on a ground of red. There is a company of Siamese musicians on board; and as we have drifted along through the bright atmosphere of the Gulf of Siam, the men have been singing. The song is monotonous, strange, and wild. Over and over again, the

DRIFTING UP THE MEINAM IN MAY.

men have sung it or howled it. It has made me nervous, and yet there are some sweet passages in it.

"What is it all about?" I asked the captain.

"They are to sing it on some great occasion of State in Bangkok. It is an ode."

"To whom?"

"To the White Elephant."

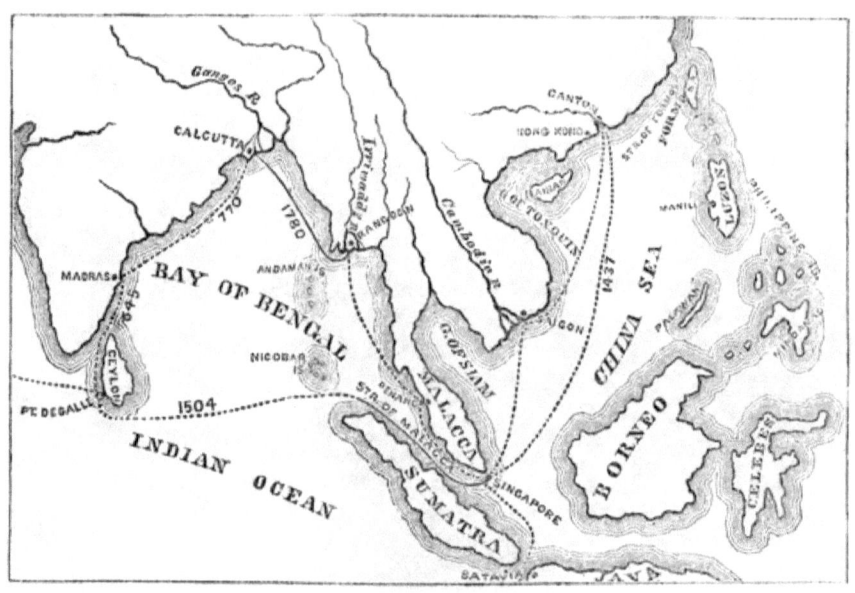

"To whom are they to sing it in Bangkok?"

"To him."

"The King, — the royal family?"

"No, no, to *him*. It is a hymn to *him*."

"Who is *him?*"

"Why, the *Elephant*, to be sure."

"The Elephant! But why should they sing to an elephant?"

"He is sacred."

"Why sacred?"

"Buddha himself was once an elephant."

"But I thought he was a teacher."

"So he was; but in his transmigration he was once reborn as an elephant. The elephant was one of the stages of his spiritual progress up to the highest manhood and to divinity."

I cannot describe to you the splendor of this tropical afternoon. The Gulf is a glimmer of light, and the air is like a great ocean of transcendent brightness. The sky seems of infinite height, with here and there the white fragment of a cloud drifting aimlessly like a wandering bird. The jungles are in full view, and we are sailing near the shore. The feathery plumes of the areca palm give a fanciful appearance to the shore, and here and there a bamboo house on poles excites the attention of an English family on board.

"Do people live in the air here?" asks one of the English children.

"Yes," answered the mother, "and in the sea too. Look!"

A house on a raft comes drifting by. From time to time a lofty structure flashes into the sun and disappears behind the curtain of the foliage. It is a temple. Boats multiply. There is a strange glimmer in the air afar. A bald-headed priest in an orange scarf points toward the dazzling light and says, "Bangkok."

On the banks of the stream I have just seen two graceful white pelicans watching for fish. I took out my revolver and pointed it at one of them, when the bald-headed priest very gently laid his hand upon mine.

"Why?"

"Why?" I could not answer. Why did there rise within me the desire to shoot the white pelican? Why? Because I was an American. But I was the son of a missionary, and I felt a sense of humiliation at being reproved by a Buddhist priest. I must make some answer, and so I said confidently, "For the same reason that the pelican seeks the life of the fish."

"Are you a pelican, my boy?"

I shook my head. The boat glided along, leaving the pelican alive and the priest's face serene and happy. The English family smiled at the episode.

"The old priest means well," said I, "but I didn't come here to learn morals from a heathen."

"We should always be willing to learn morals from those who have better morals," said the English lady. "Missionaries can teach the Siamese a better spiritual, moral, and social life. They should do so, as your father is doing. The Gospel is needed nowhere more than in Siam. The women need it, the children need it, the future needs it. But if we find anything in Siamese life that teaches a kinder heart than ours, we should accept it; for truth is truth, wherever found."

HE "POINTS TOWARD THE DAZZLING LIGHT AND SAYS, 'BANGKOK.'"

I am not sorry that I left the pelican alive.

We drift along. The musicians are singing again. I recall now that my father used to tell me about the songs to the White Elephant, but I never heard one before. I also recall that I used to hear my father say, "All life here is sacred; you must not kill anything, my son. It would hinder me in my work."

The afternoon grows more glorious. The air is luscious. The current is swift, and the tide is rising. Airy forests — oh, how beautiful! — cover the distant landscapes, and immense fern-leaves border and fringe the shores.

We have passed near the shore on the high tide, and have had an amusing experience with a gray-whiskered patriarch of a monkey and his family. He came down the trees within a stone's-throw of the ship, and began to imitate things that he saw the crew doing; and his tribe or family, a dozen or more in number, in turn imitated him. I looked at him through my hands doubled like a telescope barrel; he tried to do the same, and the others followed. I bowed to him, making a face. He nodded his head and outdid me at a grimace, as did all the rest. I tossed an orange toward the shore, but it fell into the water. This he could not imitate; but in return he made a face at me, as did all. It was a comical sight. The captain came on deck smoking a cigar. The old ape saw it, and seizing a stick broke off a part of it and put it into his mouth. The others followed. I was amused.

"Wait a minute; I'll fix them," said I. I had in my valise some Chinese powder-crackers of large size, sometimes called in America cannon crackers. I handed several of these to the crew, and lit the long fuse of the one that I held in my hand.

"Put the crackers in your mouths like cigars," I said to my friends. "I am going to toss this on shore to the monkeys."

I threw the lighted cracker shoreward, and the old ape ran down the trees and rescued it from the very verge of the water. He ran with it up into the trees, and seemed delighted.

"Now!" said I.

My friends and myself put the unlighted crackers into our mouths like cigars. The old ape did the same in a very happy state of mind. The other apes imitated him with broken sticks. The fuse burned slowly, and the old ape and his followers seemed not a little nervous at the smell of the hemp. Our interest grew intense; and the monkeys, too, as by a kind of nervous sympathy, seemed excited. Just then the old priest lifted his head above the deck, and saw what we were doing.

"My boy!"

It was too late. The monkeys were seated in a row, and seemed to be a little sceptical that all might not be quite right.

Bang! The transformation was like lightning. If ever living beings vanished in the twinkling of an eye, it was then. The old ape at first dropped as though shot; then uttered a cry, for his face must have been burned and his eyes were filled with smoke. The others never stopped a moment to see his fate. They went out of sight in a dozen or more long dark streaks. The cries of the old ape were most pitiful to hear.

"You have injured his eyes," said the bald-headed priest. "Ah! he will never enjoy these beautiful scenes again. You have robbed him, my boy. Those eyes,—who gave them? You cannot give them back. The jungles,—who gave them to him? Can you make him see them as before? Sight was his; 't was his right. You had no right to deceive him; his soul was once a man's like yours."

"No right to deceive a monkey?" I said.

"No; you have no more right to deceive an animal than a child. Where were you born?"

I declare I was ashamed to tell him, he looked so sincere, benevolent, and heart-broken.

A PATRIARCH OF A MONKEY AND HIS FAMILY.

"Poor fellow! poor fellow!" said he, referring to the monkey. "All this beauty made for him, and perhaps he is all darkness now, — all gone. Poor fellow! poor fellow!"

It made my conscience burn like fire. I do not know that I permanently injured the old ape's sight. I only meant the act for a joke, and had no evil intention. I said so; but the sorrowful priest only said, —

"That will not help his eyes."

"THE MORNING WILL FIND US IN BANGKOK."

I instinctively felt that the old priest was right. Why should I delight to deprive any living being of its natural rights or enjoyments?

It is now twilight, a blaze of splendor; temples are shining afar, and now — oh, how suddenly! — the shadows are falling and people are lighting the lamps. Night comes as it were at once in these living atmospheres; the tropic sun is extinguished like a torch. I can feel the cool breath of the great trees of the shore, though the jungle is already darkness. The stars are appearing. They are like electric stars. They seem to hang in the deep, pure air. And now appears a wonder. The trees along the shore, every few minutes, seem to be illuminated as though covered with little stars; then they are dark again. I watch these strange trees. I hear the sound of night-birds and trumpet beetles. Then the trees blaze again like a cloud of fire. Now they are dark. "What is it?" you ask. So did I when I first saw the wonder when a boy. Fireflies, — armies of fireflies. They obey their leader like an army; when he gives the signal they all shine. High towers are glimmering under the stars. There is a great circle of glimmering lamps and the odor of cocoanut oil. Here and there are dark masts. Here boats with music and merry voices; there houses in the air with twinkling lamps and liquid music. The morning will find us in Bangkok.

I should enjoy it all better were I sure that I had not injured the poor old monkey's eyes. The priest is now looking at me under the lamplight. He evidently regards me as a monster. Am I so bad, or is it because he is a heathen? Really, I do pity the poor old monkey. No philosophy will help him if I have injured him, which I hope I have not. Good-night.

CHAPTER IV.

A CITY RULED BY AN ELEPHANT.

THE next letter that I received from Cousin Ivory related to Bangkok, the great city of Siam; and its incidents of animal life were still more novel and wonderful. Could I believe it, — a great city of modern date governed by an elephant!

"The flag of the White Elephant floats over me," he said, "and I am now in a city of Buddha whose god is the White Elephant. In fact, the White Elephant may be said to govern the city, for the two kings themselves worship him. The priests bow down to him, and the people approach him on their knees. Queerly enough, I might almost truly say that in this city the animals rule.

Why the White Elephant? In the many transmigrations of the soul of Buddha, in his long journey to the regions of perfect bliss and peace, he was, according to the Buddhist myths, once reborn as a white elephant. This birth indicated great progress in the spiritual life. Hence the White Elephant is believed to be the rebirth of some great and noble soul, in its stages of progress towards the blissful state where all desires shall end in perfect peace. For, you know, the Buddhists believe that men are reborn according to merit. A bad man might be reborn as one of the meanest and most despised of animals; a man of some virtues and some evil habits, as a common animal: but a man who had made progress or merit in this life would be reborn, if an animal at all, as a very noble animal; and the noblest animal on earth, according to the Buddhist, is the White Elephant, because Buddha himself, in his progress, was once a white elephant.

But in what sense, you ask, may the White Elephant be said to rule this beautiful city?

The Buddhists believe in *merit*, or what we would call good deeds. The easy way of obtaining merit is by offerings to idols and idol-temples; and no merit-worship, to the Siamese, can be more delightful than that of the White Elephant. *Merit* is believed to be the means of spiritual progress in another world, or to a rebirth in a higher sphere.

So the flag of the White Elephant floats over the tropical city, buried in graceful palms and trees. So the great festivals of the city are those of the White Elephant; and kings and princes approach the stables of the White Elephants with awe, and the people gain *merit* by their offerings to the noble beasts. Bangkok is, or was, the City of the White Elephant.

"FOR. YOU KNOW, THE BUDDHISTS BELIEVE THAT MEN ARE REBORN ACCORDING TO MERIT."

All animals are sacred here, as I have said, for they are believed to be but the rebirth of souls. The friendship between men and animals is something beautiful, apart from the superstition from which it arises. I have often asked, Why should not this spirit prevail everywhere without superstition? I am not turning Buddhist, but I have been made to see here that there is something that makes men better in friendly relations with animals.

Take my arm, Marlow, and we will visit the city in fancy, and I will go with you in my recollections to the places I have visited, and we will at last pay our devotions to his Majesty the White Elephant. We will start by water; for Bangkok is like Venice, and the Broadway of the city is the placid Meinam, where boats are as thick as vehicles in New York.

The great wat, or temple, rises like a mountain of gold over all. There are some two hundred temples in the city, but this is the temple of temples. How its tiles shine in the clear air, and its front blazes with gold! It covers a colossal image of Buddha. See the yellow-robed priests as we pass!

THE ELEPHANTS' KRAAL.

"Their heads are shaved," you say. Yes; and their eyebrows, too. There used to be ten thousand priests in the city, all dependent on charity; but their numbers are less now, and will be less in the future.

Mark the boats in the river, like carts on a street! See the market-boats, loaded with vegetables; see the little boats of the children!

And the flags, — how beautiful they are in the tropic sunshine! Which is the handsomest? The English? No. The Tricolor? No. The White Elephant? No. The Stars and Stripes? Yes; and we would say so were we not Americans. The sails of commerce bear the Cross, and it is *that* flag that is changing Siam. It is the spirit and meaning of that flag that will one day crumble the temples and cause superstition to fade away.

See the floating houses! Was there ever so strange a city? Venice has water streets, but not floating dwellings. It is true they are anchored, but they rise and fall with the tide. Sometimes a house loses its anchorage, or its post, and drifts away up or down the river. It must be an odd thing to lose one's house in such a way, — for a man to come home to his family and find his house gone up the river.

And floating restaurants! Let us stop and take a meal. What shall it be? Steaks; fowl; hot rice; all manner of fruits and vegetables.

The wonders increase. What glittering temples rise out of the green billows of trees! Picturesque Chinese meet our eyes everywhere, — going to trade, perhaps. The Chinese have a bazaar which is said to be a mile long.

Now we are near the palace. It is enclosed by a wall about a mile in circumference. Near it are the palaces of the White Elephants.

"Never mind the King and his palace," I hear you say. "Let us leave our boat and visit the elephants."

But the palace itself is a wonder, not so much in its splendor as in its extent. It is a town of palaces; and the harem itself, where the wives of the King live, is also a town. The area of land within the palace walls comprises nearly fifty acres, and within it lives a household of more than five thousand persons. The former kings had hundreds of wives, but with the progress of Eastern ideas the royal household has diminished.

The stables, or palaces, of the White Elephants are near the palace, — a block of buildings near the arsenal. Each elephant has his own apartment, with attendants and grooms who never leave him, day or night. The apartments are lofty; and at one end is an image of Buddha, with lamps continually burning before it. Over the door of each apartment is the name of the elephant, and his royal titles.

The royal beast stands on a pedestal. He is not white, but of a dusky gray color. He has rings of gold on his tusks, and is fastened to a golden post by ropes covered with crimson.

But what is about to happen? Men are approaching him with silver salvers on their knees. On the salvers are bananas and sugar-cane and luscious fruit. He proudly takes these offerings from the creeping human beings, who feel that they have made merit for another world.

Again they approach him! This time with small bundles of grass in silver dishes. He receives it as before. More merit! The celestial world grows brighter to the fancy of the creepers, for all these deeds. Buddha must love them all, for was he not once an elephant?

He has eaten! Now one of the devotees raises a long iron comb and scratches him. More merit! Another wipes his eyes. He is given a sponge-bath many times a day.

When the King comes to visit and worship him, he trumpets. There was recently placed in the stables a very democratic young elephant, that trumpeted when any well-dressed stranger came to visit him. He evidently had caught the spirit of progress.

The population of Bangkok is some half-million of souls, nearly one half of whom are Chinese. It is a city of gardens, temples, and palaces, of floating houses, and of simple dwellings innumerable, with airy balconies buried in palms and trees. Most of the latter are made of bamboo, and roofed with the leaves of the atap palm. The walls of the city describe a circumference of some five miles.

Let us ascend to an elevation of about one hundred feet, and look down upon the swarming city and river and canals. At first it looks like a tropical forest. The foliage is the richest in any city on earth. Cocoanut-trees, betel, palmyra, tamarind, mingle their greenery, flowers, or fruit; and we see through them the great hive of human life, as one sees the apiary through a garden. The glistening river seems to form the letter S. It swarms with water-craft. The temples rise out of the garden of the city, and shine in the pure air. Beautiful, beautiful, is Bangkok, the City of the White Elephant!

Ivory's next letter was even more interesting; it described —

"THE PALACE ITSELF IS A WONDER."

HOW THEY ENTRAP THE WHITE ELEPHANTS IN SIAM.

One bright, sunny morning in that most delightful of all months in India, the cool month of November, 1862, a report was brought into the royal palace of Bangkok that a white elephant had been seen in the forest of Ayudhya.

If an angel had appeared in the midst of the royal household, or if a star had fallen from its place in the heavens, they could not have expressed more frantic delight. As I was going quietly to my school-room table on that eventful morning, a number of my little pupils rushed up frantically to me, crying, "He is come, he is come! Oh, oh! How nice, how nice!"

"Who is come?" said I, thinking it must be a great prince from some distant country.

"The White Elephant, the White Elephant, our dear guardian angel!" echoed all the voices at once. It was impossible to repress a smile. But the joy was not confined to the royal household alone. The glad news spread like wildfire over the country; and King and peasant, master and slave, young and old, even the old dames and little toddling infants of a year old, took up the good news and proclaimed it from place to place, crying, "Chang poouk ma loa, Chang poouk ma loa!"—"The White Elephant has come, the White Elephant has come!" Prayers and offerings were immediately made in all the temples; and the town-crier, who shouted the wondrous fact to the people, had offerings of money, cloth, rice, and oil made to him.

Seventy-five royal barges and a hundred boats, filled with members of the King's family, Amazons, etc., with provisions for a week's stay, were made ready that very evening. I also solicited permission to join the royal party; and before sunset we were all off, amid firing of guns, and shouts of the people from far and near, to see the precious beast entrapped and brought in triumph to the city of Bangkok, where he was looked upon as a guardian angel sent from heaven to the kingdom which is called, after him, the Kingdom of the White Elephant.

My young readers must know that there is near the forest of Ayudhya, a spot prepared for entrapping wild elephants of all kinds, which are afterward trained for hunting and war, and also for travelling through the mountains and unexplored regions round about Siam. This place is called a kraal, and is formed of heavy piles of wood driven into the ground, in a circle from three to four miles in extent.

On the south of the kraal at Ayudhya were a number of buildings raised about twenty-five feet above the ground, the lower part being entirely composed of strong posts, where the elephant-hunters live, and whence they traverse the forest at stated seasons in quest of wild beasts, such as the rhinoceros, the wild boar, wolves, panthers, tigers, and wild elephants, which abound in them. On the north side there was erected a temporary palace for

DRIVING WILD ELEPHANTS INTO THE KRAAL.

the King and his party, who generally came out here once a year to see the sport.

Only a few large trees are allowed to occupy the space enclosed for a kraal; the ground is cleared, and made perfectly hard and dry, and the piles are driven in so closely, and are so strong, that they withstand the most furious exertions often made by the beasts, when caught, to tear them up. The opening to the kraal is a very curious contrivance. When the wild beast pushes against it on the outer side, it gives way at once; but from the inner side, the more it is pressed against, the more invincible it becomes.

After leaving our boats at the city of Ayudhya, next morning we rode some miles on horseback, through a beautiful country, to the spot where the kraal stands, accompanied by a great retinue, with flags flying, drums beating, and

ROYAL AUDIENCE HALL AT BANGKOK.

heralds on horse going before to clear the royal way. Fortunately it was a clear day, and we could see a great distance. Arrived at the King's palace, we mounted a steep flight of stairs that led us to a pavilion, or open tower, about two hundred feet from the ground, whence we could command a magnificent view of the wide country about us. Adjoining the tower was a large chamber, which held nothing but one huge drum; and round it we stationed no less than twelve men, who struck it simultaneously with immense drum-sticks.

Right in front of the pavilion below, were ranged, in regular order, a hundred and fifty hunting elephants, and on each were seated two men,—one at the back, the driver, with his long goad, or forked spear, in his hand, to urge the beast to the onslaught; and the other the hunter, armed with lances, spears, and a quiver attached to his seat, full of arrows, ready to be discharged at a moment's notice.

The moment this formidable-looking hunting-party saw the royal assembly, they wheeled round, and formed a semicircle; then each hunter raised aloft his spear and saluted the King. After which each of the drivers gave the word of command in a deep, loud voice to his elephant to do the same to the King. No sooner was the word spoken than each beast lifted its heavy trunk in the air, and brought it solemnly down to the earth. I never saw a more comical sight than this elephant salutation to the King of Siam.

This done, the colossal drum from the adjoining chamber thundered out the signal for the hunt to begin. Away went the mighty company of hunters, one half on one, and one half on the opposite side, darting off in a semicircle to scour the forest where the White Elephant had been seen grazing with a troop of black ones.

It was a very exciting sight,—these elephants now appearing, now disappearing through the trees, the drivers goading them on, and the hunters all ready, spear in hand, prepared to strike. Round and round they careered, each time decreasing the circle of their movements, and hemming in the wild beasts into a smaller and smaller compass.

Now we could see them distinctly, and then we could only tell where they were by their loud shouts of "Mahkhe, mahkhe!"—"Come nearer, come nearer!" Then came a terrific succession of wild yells from the beasts, followed by fresh cries from the hunters of "Don't let them escape! don't let them escape!" which were lost almost as soon as heard, amid a deafening peal of bugles and horns and trumpets.

Nearer and nearer came the troop of wild elephants, more deafening grew the shouts, till finally we could see the beasts plunging madly round and round, amid a perfect circle, formed by the hunters on their beasts. All at once, one tremendous black creature thought he saw an opening close by, made a wild bound head-foremost, and pushed through the gate of the kraal. In plunged the whole gang, shrieking, with their trunks thrown high up in the air after them; and the heavy bar, which gave way at their slightest touch, now fell back, and held about thirty furious mad beasts safe prisoners.

The hunt was over, and it was almost noon. Wherever we turned our eyes, there were the wild beasts, howling and shrieking, running hither and thither, lashing the stolid posts with their trunks, twisting them round, and trying to uproot them, but all in vain. The sun set; and the weary beasts, tired with their violent exertions, finally huddled close together with the White, or rather salmon-colored, Elephant in their midst, as if drawn together for comfort and support in their sad captivity.

The next morning the captured troop of elephants began the day with fresh and desperate efforts to free themselves. But toward the afternoon they seemed perfectly quiet. Beginning to grow faint and weak from hunger, they finally commenced to break the branches of the trees, and tried to eat the leaves.

This was a sign for the hunters and the tame elephants to go in. About sixty men, bearing fine grass, cut and prepared, and heaps of sugar-cane, — which delights elephants as much as sugar candy does any little child, — and chains wherewith to fasten them, followed the hunters into the kraal. The latter let the tame beasts loose, and, standing a little way off, offered bits of grass or sugar-cane to the poor, starving beasts.

In a moment they all flocked round these men, and began to feed. If any of them showed any symptoms of impatience, or snatched the food too greedily from the hunter's hands, he withheld the dainties, and dealt them fierce blows instead. In less than half an hour these wild beasts of the forests took what was given to them without snatching, and were seen even to fondle with their long trunks the hands that fed them. Meanwhile the men fastened the chains to each of their right legs, and bound the wild to the tame elephants.

The White Elephant, alone, was not bound to another of its kind, but had several long silken cords fastened about his neck, and these were tied to one of the almost immovable posts of the kraal. Moreover, cakes were given to him, in addition to the grass and sugar-cane. While he was being fed, it was amusing to hear the exclamations of delight that broke from the royal party, such as, " Dear angel, gracious darling, how good, how lovely of you to come to us!"

Whereas the "gracious darling" was devouring cake after cake, utterly unconscious of the tender regard which he inspired, and quite ready to bound off, at a moment's notice, to the forest whence he had been entrapped. As soon as the White Elephant was captured, a wide path was made for him through the Country which he must traverse on his way to Bangkok; a cloth of gold was laid on his back, and off we started, in the wake of the white beast. Even the King himself had to "play second fiddle" to the new divinity.

In front of *him*, young girls danced, and sung, and played on musical instruments every step of the road; a number of men performed feats of strength and skill, tumbling and wrestling, and knocking each other about for the creature's amusement; some fanned him, others fed him, still others prayed for him, till he reached the banks of the lovely Meinam. Here he was put on board a barge, — a proceeding he did not seem to like at all, in spite of the gorgeous roof that overshadowed him, hung with crimson curtains, and literally carved with mottoes, which this learned beast was supposed to decipher with the utmost ease.

The floor of the barge was a matting curiously woven into strange patterns, and all gilt. In the middle of this the four-footed lord was placed; and round him were scattered a perfect medley of attendants, who perfumed him, sang to him, fanned him, and praised him all the way to the capital. All round his barge were the royal barges; and

THE KING AS A BOY.

silken cords, fastened to the White Elephant's vessel, were placed in the hands of nobles and the King, who thus, with their own hands, aided to float him down the river.

Thus, with shouts of joy, beating of drums, sounding of trumpets, and booming of cannon, the splendid white beast was brought to the city of Bangkok, and conducted to a pavilion prepared for him. Here a great company came out to meet him and see him receive his title. A number of Buddhist priests first offered up a prayer, then, taking a chank-shell, they poured consecrated water on his head, and named him "Phya Sire, Wongse det Sarallie Krasat," — "Glorious hero, descendant of kings and gods." Gold rings were put round his tusks, and a gold chain was hung round his burly neck; besides which, he had a beautiful purple velvet cloak, fringed with scarlet and gold, to throw over him.

Thus he was pampered and petted for seven long days; and before the new royal stables that they were building for him could be got ready, the poor beast, unable to bear all that was heaped upon him fell sick one night and died.

No man dared to tell the King the awful tidings. When he came out to look at the new stables, what was his astonishment to find the place where it stood empty! The prime minister had set thousands of workmen to pull it down in the night. The truth flashed upon the poor King, and, with a cry of pain, he sank down upon a stone and began to weep bitterly. One of the children, who had been instructed what to say, knelt before the King, and said, "Weep not, O my father. The stranger lord may have left us but for a time." The poor stranger lord had died of eating too many cakes, which had brought on a dreadful fit of indigestion.

A few days after the death of the White Elephant, I went to see the King. He did nothing but talk of the sad end of their beloved guardian angel. He showed me a piece of its skin, which he had preserved, and his tusks, which, in size and whiteness, certainly surpassed any that I had ever seen. After which he read me a description of the dead monster: "His eyes were light blue, surrounded by a beautiful salmon color; his hair fine, soft, and long; his complexion pinkish white; his tusks like long, white pearls; his ears like silver shields; his trunk like a comet's tail; his legs like the feet of the skies; his tread like the sound of thunder; his looks full of meditation; his expression full of tenderness; his cry like the voice of a mighty warrior, and his whole bearing that of an illustrious monarch."

Such is the veneration in which a white elephant is held in Siam. And such is the dreadful power of superstition, that it blinds us to what is palpably before our very eyes; for, in truth, "these people have eyes, but they see not."

CHAPTER V.

AYUTHIA, THE TERRESTRIAL PARADISE.

AMONG the splendid cities of the earth that have come and vanished like an Oriental dream, is the royal city of Ayuthia, the old residence of the rich and mysterious Siamese kings. Few cities were ever more splendid in the days of their glory, and few splendid cities are to-day more unknown. The old city of kings rose in a mist of romance, behind which the dazzling light of poetic genius shone and glowed.

There was, according to the old poetic tradition, an old King of Siam, who, finding that the world was vanity and that all things were passing by him and leaving him to physical ills and death, used to retire to the mountains for meditation and prayer. One day, while in the solitudes, there appeared to him a beautiful Queen; and his heart, which he deemed dead to love, was enamored of her beauty.

"Who are you?"

"The Queen of the Underworld."

"Let us wed."

"But I must return to my people, the Nakhae."

"Nevertheless, let us wed. I will put on your finger this ring."

So the aged King wedded the Queen of the Underworld; and after a time the Queen descended to her own people and did not often revisit the regions of the sun and air.

Time passed, and the King and priests received a message from Gaudama. It was like this: "An heir to the throne shall come mysteriously to the palace, and shall be the most glorious of kings." So the realm waited the appearance of this mysterious Prince.

One day a hunter discovered in a forest a strange and beautiful boy. He brought him to the palace. As the boy entered the gates the whole palace trembled. The King received the youth with awe, and his eye caught sight of a beautiful jewel on his hand.

"What have you there?" asked the King.

The youth outstretched his hand; and the King beheld the ring that he had given to the Queen of the Underworld, and he knew that the heir announced by Gaudama had come.

The youth was Phra Ruang, the Siamese Solomon. He became King, married the daughter of the King of China, introduced the alphabet, and wrote the ancient history of the race. His departure was as mysterious as his advent. "I must go to the river," he said one day.

As Egypt is the gift of the Nile, so Siam is the child of the glorious river which renews its youth year by year. The King went to the river and vanished from mortal eyes. They waited his return, but he never came. Then they said, "He has gone from the sun to the land of his mother."

Such was the brilliant myth that begins the rise of the royal city of Ayuthia, a few centuries after the Christian era. The city grew, and palaces and temples spread their golden wings, and silver spires seemed to reach the stars, and golden domes to hang in the sky. Dynasties of splendid kings came and went; except to a few priests, their names are forgotten sounds. Then the city was founded again in solemn state, and it now ruled the isles of the sea. More splendid palaces rose, in one of which was an image of Buddha of pure gold which weighed one hundred and forty-one thousand pounds. Another image of Buddha was fifty cubits high.

"THE ROYAL CITY OF AYUTHIA."

There was an airy bridge in the grand old city; over it passed countless millions of feet long vanished and as forgotten as the long effaced waves of the sea. The bridges of all great cities have been places of romances and tragedies, and this bridge had its historic episode which became a national tale.

King Intharaxa had three sons. The two eldest became rulers of provinces during the latter part of their father's life, and each expected the throne. The third son had no such expectation. He lived like a Prince, in quiet, well knowing that his brothers' lives and ambitions rose like walls between him and the royal power. King Intharaxa died, and the two brothers heard of his death in the provinces. Each mounted a royal elephant and hurried toward the palace. They met upon the bridge. Each knew the purpose of the other, and each determined to kill the other and thus make sure his claim to the throne. The fight began — on the war elephants, as we may suppose — on the bridge. In the contest each inflicted upon the other a mortal wound, and there were a dead King and two dead Princes and a vacant throne. The city was filled with horror and awe when the quiet third brother came forward and brought to the throne an unambitious heart. His reign was long and prosperous, and among the golden years of the royal city.

Kings succeeded kings again, and royal romances added chapter to chapter of old Siamese history. Canals were built in the royal city, — water streets, — and the city became like Venice. The wonder grew, and the city was called the Terrestrial Paradise.

Three hundred temples and palaces led the eye away toward the burning horizon. In the long river were not only floating houses but bazaars. Just outside of the city rose a pyramid called the "Golden Mountain," in which were an image of Buddha and an altar to Buddha, overhung by a dome which seemed suspended from the air.

The old city of Ayuthia is now a ruin. Its ancient palaces are buried in shrubs and trees. Out of the dense tropical foliage pinnacles and domes still rise, and some of them still glitter in the clear blue sky, but they are filled with bats. The broken shrines are the homes of bats. Where millions of human beings bowed and worshipped in some of the most splendid ceremonies that the sun ever saw, are now millions of bats. Gaudama is a vanished god, where once jewelled priests in long processions chanted his praises. Yet the many truths that he uttered still live, and will ever live; for though error perishes, truth is truth wherever found. It is Gaudama's teachings that protects the bats that inhabit his own temples and multiply in his own crumbling shrines.

The history of Ayuthia is that of old Siam. In another chapter I will tell you something of Bangkok.

THE STRANGE STORY OF THE GREEK SAILOR, FALCON.

Constantine Falcon was a son of the Governor of Cephalonia. His parents were noble, but poor; and at the age of ten he became inspired with an ambition to raise his family out of their moneyless condition.

He went to sea, and was shipwrecked in the Siam River. He lay down to sleep amid the tropical airs. Just as he was about to sink into slumber, there appeared to him a majestic form.

"Return to where you were wrecked," said the mysterious person, and vanished.

Falcon obeyed the dream or vision. He beheld on the shore a strange person approaching him.

"Where are you from?" asked young Falcon.

"From a wreck."

"Who are you?"

"I am an ambassador from the King of Siam to Persia. On my way home I was wrecked on this coast. Who are you?"

"I was also wrecked on this coast," answered Falcon.

The two became friends, and agreed to travel together, and to go to the Court of Siam. They procured a boat; and thus Falcon became introduced to the nobles of Ayuthia and to the Siamese Court. Ayuthia was then in her glory, just before her period of decline. The Court was rich and splendid; and Falcon, on account of his diplomatic knowledge and accomplishments, became

RUINS OF THE GOLDEN MOUNTAIN.

a favorite of the king. The King of Siam made him the leader of his Court; and it now became Falcon's ambition to introduce Christianity into Siam, and to make the King known to the European monarchs.

He sent an embassy to Louis XIV., King of France, "The Grand Monarch." The King returned the courtesy, and the shipwrecked young Greek found himself receiving, as Prime Minister, the ambassador of the most magnificent monarch of Europe. The result of this friendship of the two Courts was the bringing of Catholic missionaries to Siam, and the procuring of a French bodyguard for the King.

Falcon was now rich, was virtually the Prime Minister of one of the most splendid kingdoms of the world; he was allowed to enjoy his own religion amid the temples of Gaudama, and he was protected by a French guard. What a dazzling position! What a transformation from the life of the poor boy-mariner!

But ambition tempted him too far; his star of destiny went down, and he fell. The French guard excited the jealousy of the Siamese nobles; and the Catholic missions met the opposition of the Mohammedans, who themselves hoped to convert the Court and King.

Falcon at last fell a victim to a conspiracy led by an officer of State, was imprisoned, and was executed at the age of forty-one. Through the strange romance of his life the Cross was borne into Siam, and the Gospel was first preached. These events took place just before the decline of Ayuthia and the rise of Bangkok.

CHAPTER VI.

THE MOST WONDERFUL RUINS OF ASIA.

"I HAVE been," wrote Ivory in his next letter, "to what has been called the most wonderful ruin in the world; and if not the most wonderful, it is one of the most mysterious. You may never have heard of Cambodia or of Chantaboon. It would not be strange, for they belong to the country on the eastern coast of Siam, and few countries have had less to do with the world.

"You have heard of the Lion Rock. It lies at the entrance of the harbor of Chantaboon,—a rock that bears such a marked resemblance to a lion that it does not seem possible that it could be an accidental image. Yet so it is. I enclose a picture.

"'I ENCLOSE A PICTURE.'"

"Some hundred or more miles inland from Chantaboon, near the great Lake of Cambodia, is Siam Rap, and near it are the ruins of Angker. Nagken Them, or Angker the Great, these ruins are sometimes called. They are to-day but wrecks of temples amid the jungles, though the outer wall, built of volcanic rocks, is well preserved.

"Angkor the Great! Who in the Western world has heard of this once vast and populous city, that in its day was a rival of Persepolis? Old tradition says it had miles of treasure-houses, — according to one writer, three hundred

THE LEPER KING.

miles; seventy thousand war elephants and six millions of foot soldiers, if we may believe the same historian; an army of tributary princes. Yet who to-day knows the name of one of these once splendid kings?

"There is a great statue of a leper king, seated on a stone platform near the gate of the inner wall. On the pedestal is an inscription. Who can read it? Yet every king of Angker the Great must have deemed his future eternal.

"The great temple, or wat, of this vanished city, through whose streets once passed millions of soldiers in triumphal procession, must have been one of the most remarkable structures in the world. The magnitude of its ruins makes one silent in wonder. It was entered by an immense stone causeway, which still remains, and through a lofty gateway guarded by gigantic stone lions hewn from a single rock. The structure rises in quadrangular tiers. Out of the central tiers rises a great tower one hundred and eighty feet high. It is supposed that Mount Menu — the centre of the universe according to Buddha — is symbolized by the temple.

"Of Mount Menu, or Meru, the author of 'Temples and Elephants' gives the following curious description: —

"'According to the Laosian idea, the centre of the world is Mount Zinnalo (called in Siamese Mount Meru), which is half under water and half above. The subaqueous part of the mount is a solid rock which has three root-like rocks protruding from the water into the air above. Round this mountain is coiled a large fish, called "Pla anun," of such leviathan dimensions that it can embrace and move the mountain; when it sleeps the earth is quiet, but when it moves it produces earthquakes.

"'Mount Zinnalo is full of caves, which under the water are inhabited by dragons called "Naks;" while those above are the home of angels, or "Thewedas." Above the earth, and around this great mountain, is the firmament, with the sun, the moon, and the stars. These are looked upon as the ornaments of the heavenly temples. It is recorded that one of Buddha's disciples once interrupted him in his lecture, and asked the master what was beyond the firmament, when the great sage simply told him to "shut up."

"'Above the water is the inhabited earth; and on each of the four sides of Mount Zinnalo are seven hills rising in equal gradations, one above the other, which are the first ascents the departed has to make. If he is wanting in "merit," he cannot get to the top; but, having got to the summit, he now comes to the different chambers in heaven.

"'The first heavenly space, immediately on the summit of Mount Zinnalo, is "Tja to maha la chee ka tawa," which is the abode of good spirits, and where also resides a king or chief called Phya Wett So'wan.

"'A step higher up is "Tawah tingsa nang tewa nang." Here live the persons who when on earth built "salas," and houses for the priests, and to each of them is allowed sixteen thousand wives. Phya In is the chief of the company here, and he receives his orders from above.

"THE TEMPLE COVERED AN AREA OF TEN ACRES."

"'The next chamber of heaven is "Tut sida tewa." The folks residing here are those who, when on earth, wore white clothing, and passed the time in saying prayers; and each of these pious individuals has thirty thousand wives.

"'Chamber No. 4 is the "Yama tewa," inhabited by both sexes, who when on earth performed works of great merit.

"'The fifth heaven is "Nimma nalatee," also an abode for good persons. Each man has six hundred thousand wives.

"'Heaven No. 6 is "Para min mitta," a home where the people have perfect peace; they spend their time in singing and dancing, and one hundred and five million wives are allotted to each gentleman.

"'Beyond this is a heaven divided into three chambers or kingdoms, each of which is subdivided again into three compartments, as follows:—

"'"Poma tewa" is for both sexes, who have more merit than "Indra."

"'"Maha pom ma," also for men and women of the highest order; here reside the four regents of heaven.

"'"Poma palo pitta," likewise for people of both sexes, whose business is to take care of heaven.

"'In the second kingdom are the three places, or highest heavens, reserved for those who have made great merit to enjoy for a season "felicity" and "glory" before going to "Nirvana;" and there are separate places for men, priests, and women.

"'In the third kingdom reside the three orders of angels, having apartments:—

"'"Theweda newa sunja," only for females.

"'"Tewa butt utang," for men only, who are the most perfect angels, and reside here before becoming gods and ruling over men, like Buddha.

"'Those who have merit to attain the third order become mothers of gods.

"'Above all is outer darkness, or "Nirvana," which Buddha is said to have compared to the disappearance of gunpowder when lighted in your hand. By some the word "Nirvana" is accordingly interpreted to mean "non-existence;" but I doubt if this is the correct interpretation.

"'According to Mr. Alabaster, who is without a doubt the highest authority on Siamese Buddhism, it is "a place of comfort where there is no care: lovely is the glorious realm of Nirvana." And I agree with Mr. Alabaster that it is a place of perfect happiness. On ancient figures of Buddha inscriptions are often found in which the maker of the image implores the aid of Buddha in reaching the "highest heaven." If the inferior heavens are the places of enjoyment described above, there would be no object in praying for removal thence to a place of non-existence or unconsciousness.'

"The legend is as strange and wonderful as the temple itself.

"Flights of stairways once led from terrace to terrace; there were long galleries of polished marble and grotesque reliefs, colonnades carved with sacred lobas, — a mountain of art opened to the bright sun and the balmy air. The bas reliefs are themselves a dead army of figures, — angels, giants and warriors, scenes of legendary and historic lore.

"Think of it. The temple covered an area of ten acres, and the courts and gardens once enclosed two hundred and eight acres.

"It was built of stone. They were brought from mountains some thirty miles away, and perhaps employed the labor of an army of men for decades or centuries. No mortar was used in the building, but the great blocks of stone were so fitted that to-day it is hard to find the seams.

"'As grand as the Temple of Solomon it must have been,' said one astonished traveller. 'It occupied a larger space than the ruins of Karnak,' writes another.

"No ruin of Egypt, Greece, or Rome is more wonderful or more mysterious. And yet Angker the Great, with its thousands of acres of buried streets and houses, is now but the part of a dense forest in an almost unknown land. It is reached through jungles, where the traveller is followed by challenging monkeys and birds. It is the habitation of innumerable bats; there are bats everywhere, as though to them were given the eternal custody of the dead city.

"How old was the city? When was it founded? How did it perish? No one knows.

"But there was a period — it may have lasted for half a thousand years — when devotees thronged the gigantic temple, when wealth filled its marts, when armies trod its streets, and when the proudest kings of earth, in long succession, sat upon its golden thrones and wore its jewelled diadems.

"Here palaces rose, shone in the sun, and fell; and thrilling episodes of court life must have happened; but all has vanished like a vision.

"'Who built these ruins?' I asked of a Siamese guide.

"'They.'

"'Who?'

"'They themselves!'

"'Giants?'

"'No.'

"'Buddha?'

"'No; men who are dust like their habitations.'

"I spent a night amid the ruins with a provincial officer, to whose care they are entrusted. It is nearly a day's journey around them; and, tired at last, I sat down after struggling amid the jungle. The blazing sunset came, and the sudden twilight. Then the half-moon arose in the clear sky. All was silent except the whir of bats.

"There was I, an American boy, alone, as it were, amid the slowly decaying walls of Angker the Great. Not one of the inhabitants of the old city ever dreamed of the country from whence I came, and few of my own countrymen ever heard of Angker, except those who had seen the specimens of its bas reliefs at Paris or photographs in the English museums. So time sweeps away men, and kings as well as men; and palaces, and temples as well as palaces. Righteousness and its fruits alone are immortal.

"Will St. Peter's and St. Paul's one day be dust? Will time so multiply heroes that the potential names of to-day will be to long generations to come at first limited, then obscure, and then unknown?

"I fell asleep in that awful solitude with a desire to give my life to all that was good, and to overcome all that was evil. Men die, but principles live; and to live for eternal principles of righteousness and charity is the only worthy thing. Have you not felt this conviction?"

THE GIANT BRIDGE AT ANGKER, RESTORED.

CHAPTER VII.

THE STORY OF THE LEPER KING.

THOUSANDS and thousands of years ago, in the Golden Age of Time, heaven was so near to earth that the gods lived in the very sight of men.

There was a mountain called Menu, or Meru, that rose from the centre of the earth and touched the Celestial Paradise, and the gods descended and ascended upon it in full view of human eyes. Angels, too, came down out of the dazzling light and mingled with mankind.

Sorrow, pain, and disease had not entered the world, but there lived in a far dark region a dragon of great and awful power, who was an enemy of mankind.

The dragon desired to send evil into the hearts of men, and to make the kings of the world his agents of evil. He desired to see mankind suffer and follow evil desires, and to fill all the bright atmospheres of life with disease and death. Heaven would then disappear from the eyes of men, for the spiritual sight would be lost.

In these long ages of bliss men lived to be a thousand years old. Death was no terror, for the City of the Gods was already in view, and sin had not darkened the glories of the spheres where mortals would become immortal and dwell in light without the material form.

The God of the Sun held his Court in the high heavens; and it was thought just, as the ages of the earth rolled on, that one of the

"ITS DOMES WERE LIKE STARS AND ITS PINNACLES LIKE JEWELS."

gods should take the form of a man and come down to the lower world and teach the people spiritual wisdom. So Somannas was born of a lovely Princess, and grew up a beautiful youth among men.

Before he began his great mission there came a celestial messenger to his mother, the Princess, who said, —

"I must take away the boy."

"Where?"

"Up to the highest heaven."

"Why?"

"That he may learn wisdom and see the rewards of virtue, and so teach men."

The Princess was a lover of good; and that her son might learn all the mysteries of the eternal rewards and happiness of a good life, she consented to let her son go.

Then there came a flash of lightning, and the messenger and the boy went back with it into the worlds of splendor out of which it came.

The boy was taken into the counsels of the gods, and was delighted and filled with ecstasy in the dazzling light, and the Paradises of the light to which the brightest things of earth were as shadows.

The gods showed him the missions of the stars that filled the regions of space, making eternal music as they moved. They also showed him the regions of darkness where dwell those who turn good into evil, and so darken their souls.

When the boy was instructed in all the mysteries of the soul, he was returned to the earth again to teach the people wisdom, that they might retain their purity, and that the visible heaven might not be lost to their view.

The gods built a palace on earth to receive the Prince; wonderfully beautiful it was, and it sprung up in a single night under the friendly light of the stars. Its domes were like stars, and its pinnacles like jewels. It was of immense extent, and its walls were like armies of silver shields. When the sun rose on the morning after it was builded by the angels, and shone upon it, it dazzled the earth and filled mankind with wonder.

Then gods came down in the night, under the stars, and planted a celestial garden about the palace, and filled it with streams and fountains. The flowers in the garden were of delightful odor, and their breath went up to heaven and wafted perfume through the abodes of the gods.

Somannas lived here, and taught the people that the secret of happiness was righteousness, and that righteousness was of its own nature immortal. And the people were virtuous, and death was only a change into a higher light and being, and all the world was happy.

There dwelt afar a great and powerful King, who heard of Somannas and his palace and the happiness of his people. He worshipped the dragon, and the dragon made him very powerful. One day the dragon said to him, —

"I have given thee power: go and visit Somannas and tempt him to worship me."

There was a gathering of elephants and chariots, and the King from the Lotus Land started on a long journey to visit Somannas and to see his palace and people.

Somannas received him joyfully, and took him into his palace; and the two Kings became bosom friends, and for a time lived happily together.

Then the great King of the Lotus Land began to talk with Somannas about things that he did not know, and a great power that he did not possess. The knowledge that had been kept from him was that of evil, and the power that he did not possess was the power of evil.

"You should have this knowledge and power; then you would know all things, and your sovereignty would be universal."

"How shall I obtain them?"

"Worship the dragon, and you shall know the secrets of all life."

The young Prince desired all knowledge and power; but he remembered the counsels of the gods, and that he had been instructed that the knowledge of evil brought unhappiness to men, and darkened

"THE KING FROM THE LOTUS LAND STARTED ON A LONG JOURNEY."

the light within them. He saw if he gained the hidden knowledge, he would lose the power of the higher knowledge, and his love of good.

"You are tempting me to ruin the world. Evil is pain, evil is disease, evil is suffering, and evil is a dark death."

"But it is new power."

"It is a poison; and the evil in thy heart shall poison thee, for thou hast tempted me."

Then the evil in the heart of the King of the Lotus Land began to poison his body. There came white spots on his flesh, and they rotted; and his body slowly turned white and dropped away; and he was shunned by all, and one day he died.

Then Somannas changed the dead King's body into stone. "Let it be a warning," he said, "to all ages, to those who would turn the heart of the young to a knowledge of evil."

By the gate of the palace he sat, the Leper King. The people gazed upon him for ages, and saw in him the effects of the forbidden knowledge, and they repeated the wise words of Somannas, —

"We are never bound by evil until we come to know it; it is true wisdom never to know. Let the youth forever remember the Leper King."

"BY THE GATE OF THE PALACE HE SAT, THE LEPER KING."

CHAPTER VIII.

IVORY IN FLORIDA.

OUR hotel was situated on the so-called Indian River, which is really an ocean lagoon, near its mouth, and amid the beautiful lake region of Florida. We usually went to Florida about the first of December; but we did not have many guests at the hotel until after New Year's. I acted as clerk of the hotel, as telegraph operator, and took charge of the education of the proprietor's children. I was very busy from January to April, but I usually had the month of December quite to myself, as the first weeks after our arrival were holidays to the children.

The mouth of the great Indian River is full of birds always. In fact, birds seem to cover it, as sea-weeds the northern rivers where they leave the sea. I have seen the steamer for Rockledge pass down the wide waters as though it were sailing through a sea of birds. The lakes also abound with birds.

The most beautiful birds of the Indian River region and the South Florida lakes are the flamingoes, the white herons, the eyrets and ibises, — birds scarcely found anywhere else in North America. The birds that fill the rivers are chiefly ducks and small water-birds. The white heron is one of the most beautiful birds in the world, — to my eye, more beautiful than the flamingo, eyret, or ibis. Its form is most graceful, and it has a pearly whiteness that glistens in the sun. No bird — not even the Florida ibis, with all its poetic associations -

is such a beautiful ornament for a parlor, a public room, a lamp or fire screen, or is more salable by the taxidermist. I used to spend a part of the month of December hunting birds, especially the heron. I knew something of taxidermy, and I did not have to seek a market in Northern bird-stores for my stuffed specimens. I was able to sell my prepared herons and ibises to the guests at the hotel.

Southern Florida in winter is full of plume-hunters, and the beautiful birds of the Indian River and Lake Region are fast disappearing to supply the American bird-stores and the French feather-market.

Ivory, on arriving in New York, came at once to Florida, for Mr. Marden was his uncle. He was a fine-looking young man, of gentle manners, quiet behavior, with a pleasant voice. There was something affectionate in his tone while speaking, that won one's good-will. His intelligence was far above that of the ordinary student or college graduate. He had received a liberal education at Boston on his former residence in America; had met very intelligent society in England and in India. His education differed from that of other boys I had met in that he had a large knowledge of the world. His reading had been the best. He knew much Oriental literature. He could speak well several languages.

He was so modest, kindly, and affectionate, that we all came to love him; even the negroes about the hotel. Wherever he went, the young and old seemed to follow him, for it was delightful to hear him talk of his travels. He never spoke ill of anybody; so every one, even the old freedmen, felt sure that he was a true friend. Mr. Marden's children were constantly hanging about him, and the negroes were continually bringing to him questions. But we never regarded Ivory as a very *strong* character.

"Yes, Ivory is a good fellow," said Mr. Marden, "but he was never born for war or temptation. He would never have scaled the Heights of Abraham."

But I had noticed that he always had the moral courage to do right. With all his affectionate and gentle ways, he could say no. The day after his arrival I showed him the white herons I had killed and stuffed the week before. There was an eyret among them, and a rare bird whose name I did not know.

"I shall get five dollars apiece for the herons," said I. "You shall go heron-hunting with me."

"But, Manton, —"

"But what?"

"In Siam we do not kill birds for their plumage."

"But you are not a Siamese."

"No; but it is a very kindly custom, and I have been influenced by it."

"Not influenced by a Buddhist superstition, Ivory."

"Not by the superstition; but if a superstition represented a truth, it would influence you, just as though you found truth in one of Æsop's fables. Æsop was a heathen, you know."

"But the Siamese and Chinese are not good to one another. How they neglect old people! Their superstitions are heartless and cruel."

"Yes; and it is the duty of Christian people to teach them a better faith and life, as father is doing. Yet the relations between men and animals are more kindly in Buddhist countries than here, even if brought about by a superstition; and there is something in the friendship of animals that tends to increase the happiness of mankind."

"Then you would not kill herons for their plumage?"

"No."

"You would not kill a bird at all?"

"No."

"Not a buzzard?"

"No; a buzzard is a very useful bird, and does the duty for which

Nature designed it. Why should I wish to kill a flamingo or a buzzard?"

"I should think that while your father has been laboring among the Buddhists, the Buddhists have been laboring with you."

"Not at all. Siam is full of beautiful birds; they make life happier. Is Florida?"

"It used to be."

"Have you seen many flamingoes this fall?"

"No."

"Many eyrets?"

"No."

"Many ibises?"

"No."

"These beautiful friends of man are all disappearing?"

"Yes."

"Can you afford to lose them? Can the State or the country afford to lose them? Can wealth or art bring to Florida anything so beautiful as a flight of ibises, or a colony of white herons among the gray mosses, or eyrets on the borders of a lagoon? And can you for a moment believe that these birds were created to be killed?"

An incident occurred soon after this conversation that caused Ivory to be much ridiculed, even by the negroes and children, among whom he had become more and more a favorite.

I had shot a beautiful heron and broken its leg. It had been dragged out of a cypress thicket by a dog, and its plumage had thus become torn and it was unfit for taxidermy. Ivory was with me when I shot the bird. I was about to kill it and throw it away as a useless specimen, when Ivory took it up very gently, for which he was severely pricked or bitten by the bird with its sharp bill.

"What are you going to do with it?" I asked.

"Oh! take it to the hotel."

BIRDS ON THE INDIAN RIVER.

The next day I chanced to go into the yard, when I saw the wounded heron in a large coop with its leg done up in a bandage.

"Who did that?" I asked of Uncle Eben, an old negro.

"Ivory, Boss."

"Ivory?"

"Yes; he's bin mendin' dat dar bird all de mornin'. An' it bit him."

"Why did he not wring its neck?"

"Dunno, Boss; Ivory am a sort of heathen. I specs he thinks birds have souls."

The heron's leg healed, and one day the bird was missing.

"Where's your heron?" I asked of Ivory.

"Gone!"

"Where?"

"Oh, to the air, sunshine, and lakes, where he belongs."

"Who let him go?"

"I."

The negroes began to speak of Ivory as "dat boy from Siam who thought dat birds had souls." Some of them, who had heard of his feats in the parlor, began to hint that he might be a "conjurer."

Hunters came to the hotel; several of them bird-hunters, who found a sale for the bird plumage to an agent for a Paris feather-store. Ivory seemed to regard these hunters with a kind of horror. They looked upon him as a "spooney." This may have hurt him, but it did not prevent him from saying again and again, "I think that the destruction of birds in Florida is wrong. It ought to be prevented by Christian sentiment and by the State law."

I once hinted to him, in presence of the children, that his views on the subject were childish and weak-minded; but he replied that most men whose lives had proved a benefit to others had cherished the same feelings in regard to the brute creation, and he related many beautiful stories in support of this assertion.

"Genius is always kind," he said, "and great thoughts are always benevolent."

I was nettled by the implied criticism, and said, —

"Do you think that you are a genius, Ivory?"

"No; but men of genius and noble thoughts are worthy of imitation, and especially by people of common gifts like myself."

Some of Ivory's stories in defence of his principles were very kind and pleasing. They were old, but he treated them in such a sympathetic way that they were none the less interesting. He used to sit on the verandas on the sunny afternoons, when the children and the negroes would gather around him. Sometimes the hunters would mingle among the curious group. He would talk to them as though he were a preacher for animals; his eye would grow bright, his cheek color, his breath be hastily drawn, and he would debate on the subject as though he were a veritable missionary to the heathen. I recall some of his stories, as well as his sympathetic manner of telling them. One was of Sir Isaac Newton and his dog Diamond; another, of Burns and the field mouse; and another, of President Lincoln and a bird that had fallen out of its nest. He used often to quote the Bird's-nest Commandment of Moses, and as often Cowper's sentiment, —

> "I would not enter on my list of friends
> . . . the man
> Who needlessly sets foot upon a worm."

Speaking of Cowper leads me to recall Ivory's pleasant version of the melancholy poet's love of his tame hares.

COWPER'S TAME HARES.

Few old English villages are better known to the lovers of wholesome reading than Olney, the place where the Rev. John Newton labored, and the poet Cowper sung.

It is situated on the river Ouse, whose waters go dimpling by land-slopes rich with herbage and dotted with cattle, by dells and dingles, by airy groves and grand old elms.

THE RIVER OUSE GOES DIMPLING BY.

The church at Olney is associated with many pleasing events of long departed years, with seasons of spiritual refreshing, with the convincing discourses of Newton, and the sweet hymns of Cowper. In many hymn-books this memorial of Christian usefulness may be found, — Olney Hymns.

The poet Cowper was subject to great depression of spirits, and his mind, so brilliant in health, was several times in his life quite overthrown. At such periods any mental exertion increased his sufferings, and books afforded him no pleasure. He therefore sought for diversion in the delightful scenes of rural life. He spent much of his time in gardening, and in embellishing his grounds by the most lovely and attractive shrubs and flowers. His poem, the " Task," is full of rural pictures. We feel, while reading it, the warm sunlight of spring; we breathe the fragrance of fields and flowers; we hear the songs of birds and the purling of sun-tipped waters. During a severe attack of his constitutional malady at Olney, a neighbor, hoping to divert his mind from dark forebodings and vexing thoughts, presented him with a young English hare. It was a timid little creature, and yet it possessed a susceptible nature, and became so docile and winsome as to gain the poet's affection. The people of Olney were warm friends of Cowper, and, seeing him pleased with the leveret, generously offered him other pets of the same species. He, however, accepted but two. In an article published in the "Gentleman's Magazine," he tells us that in the year 1774, being much indisposed both in mind and body, incapable of diverting himself either with company or books, and yet in a condition that made some diversion necessary, he was glad of anything that would engage his attention without fatiguing it.

The children of a neighbor of his had a leveret given them for a plaything. It was at that time about three months old. Understanding better how to tease the poor thing than to feed it, and soon becoming weary of their charge, they readily consented that the father, who saw it pining and growing leaner every day, should offer it to his acceptance.

He was willing enough to take the prisoner under his protection, perceiving that, in the management of such an animal, and in the attempt to tame it, he would find just that sort of employment which his case required. It was soon known among the neighbors that he was pleased with the present, and the consequence was that in a short time he had as many leverets offered him as would have stocked a paddock. He undertook the care of three, which he named Puss, Tiney, and Bess.

The English hare is a very graceful and handsome animal. It is versicolored, and its ears are longer than its head. It remains in its form or burrow during the day, but comes out in the evening twilight in search of food. It is an affectionate creature when tame, and exhibits its affection in many beautiful ways.

The three pets — Puss, Tiney, and Bess — received much of the poet's attention during his slow recovery from the effects of disease. He observed concerning them that each had a character of its own, and that the disposition of each was indicated by its countenance.

"Puss," says Cowper, "was tamed by gentle usage; Tiney was not tamed at all; and Bess had a courage and confidence that made her tame from the beginning."

Puss was Cowper's favorite, and for nearly a dozen years was a frequent companion of his shadowed hours. Bess was a comical, frolicsome creature, and died young. Cowper said that he always admitted them into the parlor after supper, where, the carpet affording their feet a firm hold, they would frisk and bound, and play a thousand gambols, in which Bess, being remarkably strong and fearless, was always superior to the rest, and proved herself the Vestris of the party. One evening the cat, being in the room, had the hardiness to pat Bess upon the cheek, — an indignity which she resented by drumming upon the old cat's back with such violence that the cat was happy to escape from under her paws, and hide.

Tiney was a surly fellow, and would bite his master if angered. The arts of persuasion and kindness produced no effect on him. He was retained as a pet only for the reason that his surliness was very droll, and, in its way, entertaining. He lived nearly nine years. "The Epitaph on a Hare," found among Cowper's minor poems, was written on the death of Tiney.

Puss was a delightful creature in every way. She would leap into her master's lap to be caressed, and would fall asleep on her master's knee. She would suffer him to take her up, and to carry her about in his arms, and had more than once fallen fast asleep upon his knee. She was ill three days, during which time he nursed her, kept her apart from her fellows, that they might not molest her (for, like many other wild animals, they persecute one of their own species that is sick), and by constant care and trying her with a variety of herbs, restored her to perfect health.

No creature could be more grateful than his patient after her recovery; a sentiment which she most significantly expressed by licking his hand, — first the back of it, then the palm, then every finger separately, then between all the fingers, as if anxious to leave no part of it unsaluted, — a ceremony which she never performed but once again, upon a similar occasion.

Finding her extremely tractable, Cowper made it his custom to carry her always after breakfast into the garden, where she hid herself, generally, under the leaves of the cucumber vine, sleeping or chewing the cud till evening; in the leaves also of that vine she found a favorite repast.

She had not been long habituated to this taste of liberty before she began to be impatient for the return of the time when she might enjoy it. She would invite her master to the garden by drumming upon his knee, and by a look of such expression as it was not possible to misinterpret. If this rhetoric did not immediately succeed, she would take the skirt of his coat between her teeth, and pull it with all her force.

Thus Puss might be said to be perfectly tamed. The shyness of her nature was done away; and, on the whole, it was visible by many symptoms that she was happier in human society than when shut up with her natural companions.

Puss became less frolicsome and attractive as she grew old, but not the less loving. It is in allusion to Puss that Cowper penned the passage in the third book of the "Task," commencing: —

> "One sheltered hare
> Has never heard the sanguinary yell
> Of cruel man, exulting in her woes;
> Innocent partner," etc.

The tender-hearted poet closes the elegant passage thus: —

> "If I survive thee, I will dig thy grave,
> And when I place thee in it, sighing, say,
> I knew at least one hare that had a friend."

The death of this welcome companion of many a bitter hour affected deeply the stricken poet. He felt that an innocent joy had left his household, that time would not replace. He wrote for "poor Puss" this Latin epitaph:

> "Hic etiam jacet.
> Qui totum novennium vixit.
> Puss.
> Siste paulisper,
> Qui præteriturus es.
> Et tecum sic reputa:
> Hunc neque canis venaticus,
> Nec plumbum missile,
> Nec laqueus,
> Nec imbres nimii,
> Conficere:
> Tamen mortuus est —
> Et moriar ego."

Cowper declared that he would not add to his list of friends one who willingly would tread upon a worm. He ever held the sportsman's amusement

COWPER'S HOUSE AT OLNEY.

in abhorrence, saying that man little knew what amiable creatures he persecuted. He frequently expresses his sympathy for the brute creation in his charming pastoral poems, for which, doubtless, we owe much to the influence of winsome little Puss.

I also recall a ballad that Ivory used to sing, that had an interesting origin. The incident that inspired the writing of it touched the hearts of two English poets.

About the year 1805 there dwelt in the district a young man of elegant tastes who loved to explore these mountain regions. He was conspicuous for his literary attainments, and greatly beloved for his gentle and amiable manners. He used to make frequent excursions among the wild mountains, and would spend whole days feasting his eye on the exhaustless beauties they afforded. He was always attended by a little terrier dog, to which he was greatly attached, and which was ever on the alert to do his master's bidding. Scott, in his ballad, calls the young man the Wanderer; and so I will call him now.

One spring day, when the streams were swollen, and the mountains were beauteous with waterfalls, birds, and flowers, the Wanderer set out on an excursion that promised unusual attractions, attended by his little favorite. He penetrated too far, or remained too long; night probably overtook him, and he lost his way. He overstepped a precipice, and was dashed in pieces.

For several months the little dog watched by the remains of his beloved master, only leaving them, it is supposed, to obtain necessary food. The remains of the Wanderer were found during the following summer, by a party of excursionists; and when discovered, the terrier was guarding them with pitying care.

The young man's name was Charles Gough.

Wordsworth, with Sir Humphry Davy and Sir Walter Scott, ascended Helvellyn in the following autumn, and visited the spot where the young Wanderer perished. Both Wordsworth and Scott were much affected by the incident; and the former composed a poem entitled "Fidelity," and Scott a poem entitled "Helvellyn" in each of which the story is very beautifully told.

As the season advanced, and the mocking-birds began to sing, and the strange brightness of the Florida atmosphere, that floods the earth as the winter days lengthen, filled the tall pines and the curtains of streaming moss, guests flocked to the hotel. Among them were many amateur hunters, — invalids who had been sent to Florida to "shoot" for their health. These used to make long excursions down the Indian River to the heronries, and return with spoils. I stuffed many of their birds for them.

Ivory exerted every influence in his power against the destruction of the birds. He used the pencil skilfully, and he drew two pictures which he tacked up in the hotel office, — pictures that told a story, and that were in harmony with his thought. One was of a dog driving home a horse for help for his drunken master who had fallen from the carriage (see Frontispiece); and another was of a young lady riding on horseback through a wood, with a stuffed bird on her high hat. The bird and the hat rose above the thicket, and a hunter in the thicket had aimed his gun at the bird, and a panther was slowly stealing up behind the hunter. It was entitled "All of a Kind."

It was always instructive to hear him talk of birds. One of his stories that used to please the negroes was about the morning dance of the Birds of Paradise in the islands of the East.

Ivory's classification of birds was novel, taken from some old and ingenious naturalist. "Birds are classified in different ways by different ornithologists," he said one day as a large group of friends had gathered around him on the veranda, and the hunters came strolling home to the hotel. "One of the most simple and ingenious classifications of birds is that of an English naturalist, based chiefly on their peculiar habits of constructing nests. He divides the more than one hundred different genera, and more than five thousand different species of birds, into twelve groups: miners, ground-builders, masons, carpenters, platform-builders, basket-makers, weavers, tailors, felt-makers, cementers, dome-builders, and parasites.

"The bank-swallows and the petrels afford familiar illustrations of the miners. The former excavate holes in the earth for their nests, sometimes three feet in depth; the latter incubate in similar holes, but under the rocks and stones of rude and stormy coasts.

"THE ORIOLES ARE WEAVERS."

"The sparrows, larks, larger sea-birds, and nearly all domestic fowls are ground-builders. The dooryard robin and the South American baker-bird are examples of the masons. The latter constructs its nest in the exact shape of a baker's oven. The woodpeckers and chickadees are carpenters. The eagles and most of the large forest-birds are platform-builders. The white-headed eagle constructs a nest that is a perfect cube, five feet on each of its sides. The nest, or platform, of the African martial eagle is capable of sustaining the weight of a man. The mocking-bird, the blackbird, and, more remarkable than either, the sociable grosbeck, — hundreds of which colonize in the different cells of the same nest, — are basket-makers.

"The orioles are weavers. The East Indian weaver and the 'Silvia sutoria' of the Orient are true tailors. The former sews together leaves with fibres of cotton, thus making a bag, which it suspends from a limb, out of the reach of the monkeys, and in which it builds a very beautiful nest. The latter sews a dead leaf to a living one, and builds its diminutive nest between the two. The goldfinches and the humming-birds are felt-makers.

"The swallows are cementers. These sylph-like creatures, whose blithe notes ripple on the morning air and ring sweetly out on the surface of the evening lake, who twitter beneath the eaves of grand old farm-houses and rear their young in roomy out-buildings, secrete a kind of glue in glands on each side of the head, and with this they are enabled to construct their truly wonderful nests.

"The lawit, a kind of swallow that frequents the surf-beaten caves on the south coast of Java, eats a glutinous seaweed, which it disgorges, and of this vomit makes a waxy nest that is edible. It is, perhaps, the most remarkable of the cementers. Its nest is about the size of a coffee-cup; and the natives who collect these nests for the market are lowered over the cliffs and enter the tremendous caverns of the sea at the peril of their lives. The lawit's nests are esteemed in certain countries as the greatest possible luxury, and are sometimes sold for double their weight in silver."

"SWALLOWS THAT FREQUENT THE SURF-BEATEN CAVES."

After this ingenious little lecture, Ivory used sometimes to be chagrined by the colored boys bringing him birds they had caught or killed, with the question, "To what class does *this* belong?" He once answered a hunter who asked him the question: "To that of the undertakers."

The ornament of the Southern groves and forests is the mocking-bird; and he possesses, perhaps, the finest musical gifts of any warbler of our own or of any other land. He imitates the song of every bird, and surpasses them all in the fulness of his flute-like melody. Audubon says that the best notes of the nightingale do not equal "the finished talent of the mocking-bird." Wilson says: "The ease, elegance, and rapidity of his movements, the animation of his eye, and the intelligence he displays in listening to and laying up lessons from almost every species of the feathered creation within his hearing, are really surprising, and mark the peculiarity of his genius. To these qualities we may add that of a voice full, strong, and musical, and capable of almost every modulation, from the clear and mellow tone of the wood-thrush to the savage scream of the bald eagle. In measure and accent he faithfully follows his originals; in force and sweetness of expression he greatly improves upon them. In his native groves, mounted on the top of a tall bush or half-grown tree, in the dawn of the dewy morning, while the woods are already vocal with a multitude of warblers, his admirable song rises pre-eminent over that of every competitor."

The mocking-bird is able to imitate all the minor sounds of Nature. In his superb rendering of the song of the thrush he will pause to mimic the bark of a dog, the crowing of a cock, or the creaking of a wheelbarrow. A stranger in the South would suppose that a magnolia grove was alive with songsters, in which, in reality, was but a single mocking-bird.

It used to be Ivory's delight to feed the mocking-birds; and a few weeks of his friendly influence served to make those of the grounds quite tame and free to come to the jessamines that shaded the verandas of the hotel.

One day a little negro brought to him a bird of very brilliant plumage that was not very common in Florida, and the usual company gathered to hear what he would say of it.

"Wat am dat?" asked the wondering darkey.

"That is a Baltimore bird."

"Has it a soul?"

"I do not know."

He then went on to explain to the little boy in a most painstaking way the wonders of this beautiful inhabitant of the air.

CHAPTER IX.

IVORY'S STRANGE STORIES.

IVORY made the Christmas in the almost empty hotel on the Indian River a very delightful one. He had a love of making people happy, that seemed to carry an atmosphere of good will and feeling wherever he went. He knew a hundred diversions; and how a young man who had lived half of his twenty-two years in Siam could have become familiar with so many ways of diverting and entertaining, was a mystery to us all.

"What shall we have on Christmas evening?" I asked him about a week before the holidays. "There are only six guests in the hotel, and others will not arrive until after New Year's. But we must include them in our holiday gathering, as three of them are children, and two invalids. What is there that one can do to entertain a miscellaneous company?"

"Oh!" said he, "make a box of puzzles; and then 'The Mysterious Guests' is a very amusing diversion. The English used to play it in Bangkok."

"How is it played?"

"The people assemble in a room for a reception. There appears a stranger at the door, who asks to be admitted. The guest is dressed to represent some character in history, poetry, or fiction. The purpose of the play is to recognize who the guest is. Thus the caller may represent, say, Sindbad the Sailor, Little Miss Flite, Blondel, Cleopatra,

Martha Washington, — any world-renowned poet, artist, or musician. He must treat with surprise and scorn those who do not rightly recognize him, and appear delighted to meet the one who rightly guesses his name and calls him by it.

"For example, suppose the character assumed to be Oliver Goldsmith.

"A man in a wig, gayly trimmed coat, and knee-breeches, appears, and bows himself in, as if expecting to meet old friends. He says, perhaps, on entering: —

> 'In all my wanderings round this world of care,
> In all my griefs, — and God has given my share, —
> I still had hopes my latest hours to crown,
> Amidst these humble bowers to lay me down.'

Or,

> 'Where'er I roam, whatever realms to see,
> My heart untravelled fondly turns to thee.'

"'How do you do, Lord Byron?' says one of the company.

"'Lord Byron! Lord Byron! I never heard of Lord Byron. You are not the friend I came to see. *You do not know me.*'

"'How do you do, Mr. Shakspeare?' says a young person who is not very well read in the dramatic poet.

"'Mr. Shakspeare! Why, Shakspeare died long, long before my time. No, *you do not know me.*'

"He quotes: —

> 'I still had hopes — for pride attends us still —
> Amidst the swains to show my book-learned skill,
> Around my fire an evening group to draw,
> And tell of all I felt and all I saw.'

"'You must have been a great traveller. How do you do, Baron Munchausen?'

"So the play goes on.

"'How do you do, my old friend, Dr. Goldsmith? I have *known* you since boyhood, and am glad to welcome you back again.'

"A mock affecting greeting and interview follows. Other characters in the same manner appear. In circles of much intelligence obscure characters may be provided for, and the company thus kept in suspense for a long time.

"Readings from the poets, accompanied with songs, are pleasing. The readings selected should be such as contain a song, like the song 'Hail to the Chief,' in Scott, or 'Araby's Daughter,' in Moore's 'Lalla Rookh.' The story of Paul Dombey may be read from Dickens, and 'What are the wild waves saying?' sung with it.

"Music, however," he continued, "is the popular entertainment, and ballad concerts that represent history and national sentiment are always pleasing. The old songs of Germany, England, Scotland, and Ireland, in costume, suggest many entertainments. Ballad concerts of imitative songs, such as 'Gayly chant the summer birds,' 'The cows are in the corn,' 'Oh, whistle, and I will come to you, my lad,' 'Whippoorwill's Song,' etc., if less instructive, are pleasing and of good influence.

"A very profitable and interesting subject for general conversation is the best books on all leading topics of literature and art, tested by the votes of its members. For example, the subject may be, 'Who are the six greatest living poets?' After an hour's discussion slips of paper are presented to all the members, and a vote is taken. 'What are the best twelve books for young people?' to be discussed and voted upon in the same way. 'What President has exerted the best moral influence upon the country?' The voting makes it very lively and interesting."

THE ASTROLOGER FROM SIAM.

"The astrologer from Siam," said Ivory, "is another very good game, and the character may be assumed by the amateur magician. He should provide himself with a flowing robe and sleeves, a tall paper hat, like an inverted cornucopia, and should have an umbrella with a very long handle, which he should carry high above his head as he enters the room. In parties or large assemblies he may appear with his face slightly bronzed or colored.

"On entering the room, a confederate asks with seeming surprise, —

"' Who are you?'

"' I am Moonsee, the astrologer from Siam.'

"' What brings you here?'

"' I come to recover lost treasure. When we bury treasure in Siam, we despatch a slave, that his spirit may watch over it, and if it should be stolen, reveal to the Wise Men where it has gone. There is stolen treasure here to-night; I have come to recover it.'

"' But, Moonsee, where is your authority? How do we know but that you are an impostor?'

"' True, true,' putting down his umbrella, and striding about in his flowing robes. 'Do you see that coin? Examine it. It shall be a sign.'

THE ASTROLOGER FROM SIAM.

"Moonsee places the coin against the side of the wall, rubbing it up and down carelessly, and says, 'Spirit of the murdered Crow Shoon, hold the coin against the wall.'

"The coin remains on the wall as Moonsee withdraws from it.

"MOONSEE CAN BURN WATER."

"' Did you ever see a coin stick against a wall before?' he asks, and answers: 'No, never. Do you doubt my authority longer?'

"' Yes,' answers the confederate. 'That is not sufficient; I must have some further proof of your commission.'

"The rubbing of a coin, a cent or a ten-cent piece, against a smooth perpendicular surface, as the panel of a door, will generally cause it to stick by friction. If the surface of the coin be a little smooth, it will make the experiment more sure. Moonsee *rubs* the coin up and down on the surface of the door or wainscoting before he leaves it to the spirit of the 'murdered Crow Shoon.'

"Leaving the coin on the wall, Moonsee now says, 'Not satisfied yet? Well, well! you burn air in this country, I see, but you cannot burn water. No, no, but Moonsee can burn water.' He calls loudly, 'Crow Shoon! Crow Shoon!'

"Moonsee fills a lamp with water from the pail or faucet, or asks one of the party to do so. He then says, 'Wick? wick? There is no wick. Ah, I will use *ice* for wick. Never the like was seen in this country before.'

"He causes some ice to be brought to him, breaks it, and places upon the water what *looks* to be a piece of the ice, but which is really a piece of transparent camphor gum, which he has brought with him for the purpose. He lights the camphor gum, and apparently the ice and the water burn.

"Leaving the burning water, he says, 'Now I will search among you for the lost treasure, for surely you never saw water burning like that, and you must be convinced of my commission.'

"' No,' says the confederate. 'Not yet. We must have one more test. You must be able to tell us what is in our minds, and something that only we ourselves can know. Do this, and we will let you search for the treasure.'

"Moonsee walks or strides about the room, rubbing his face as in great perplexity, and then calls, 'Crow Shoon! Crow Shoon!'

"Moonsee asks for a sheet of paper. He cuts the sheet into little pieces, and asks each person present to write upon a piece of the paper three numbers: as ten, fifteen, twenty-five, or any like figures. Moonsee now asks for a package of envelopes (which has previously been put into some convenient place for the occasion), and requests each person to add the three numbers together, to place them in one of the envelopes, seal the envelope, and lay it upon the table.

"The table is provided before the performance with a plate, and on it is set a lamp to prevent its disturbance. Under the plate is an envelope, with three added numbers on a paper inside. Moonsee gathers up the envelopes, and says,—

"'I will now give an envelope to one of the best mathematicians in the room. He shall open it, and read the contents, and show it to each of you. I will then uplift my right arm, which is now as you see white, and the number in the envelope will appear in black figures upon it. But I will first have to burn the envelope, after it has been examined, in this plate.'

"Moonsee removes the lamp, and in so doing, takes up his own prepared envelope unseen from under the plate, and hands this to one of the best mathematicians in the room. The mathematician opens the envelope, reads the number, and shows it to all, then crumples it up and places it on the plate to be burned. He may burn it himself. Moonsee rubs the ashes of the burnt envelope upon his arm, lifts his arm, and the correct number appears in jet black.

"The number — as, for example, eight, seventy-five, or five hundred — has been written on Moonsee's arm in glycerine, before the performance. He shows his arm without the number, as the dried glycerine is invisible. On rubbing the ashes on his arm, the invisible glycerine figures immediately appear, to the astonishment of all who see the transformation.

"Moonsee now proceeds to search the company. He finds parts of the lost treasure on the persons of all present,— curious articles and coins, which he has already in his sleeve or palm, for use. He seems to pull these out of the pockets of the company. Every one is found to have stolen treasures on his person.

"At the close the confederate explains all, and says, 'We must look upon wonders with the eyes of reason rather than those of the head. Prove all things. Good-night, Moonsee.'"

Ivory made suggestion after suggestion, and at last said, "If you wish me I will tell on that evening some holiday stories that I learned in the East."

I was pleased. I was sure that Ivory's stories and experiments would be most acceptable to us all, and very novel; and so I posted at the hotel desk, "Siamese Stories and Novelties in the Parlor on Christmas Eve."

THE MYSTERIOUS FAKIR, OR A CHRISTMAS EVE IN A ZENÄNA.

I shall never forget a Christmas which I spent with my aunt at Maulmain on my return from America to Siam. It was in a house the back court of which had once been a zenäna, and where some native Christian women still lived. I was walking to and fro in the court which opened out of the zenäna. A light breeze broke the stillness of the air, and a shower of blossoms came drifting down at my feet. A cocoanut-palm threw its shadow across the wall of the half-open paved court, and on the wall under the palm sat a peacock and a monkey, each seemingly unconscious of the presence of the other. Whence the shower of blossoms came, I could not tell. Not from the cocoanut-palm, sure, but drifting from the unknown trees that rose like domes of bloom everywhere in the air.

"Look at these blossoms!" I said. "Just like a snow-storm in the North, or a shower of apple-blossoms in an old American orchard. The day before Christmas, too! Just look at that monkey!" said I. "See how he follows me with his eyes, and turns his head like a weather-vane in whichever way I go. He just now winked at me."

"Look well to your valuables!" said my aunt, with an amused expression, "or you may lose them and lose sight of the monkey at the same time. When I lose sight of the monkey I usually lose sight of something else, and I always look around me to see what is gone."

"Do you observe Christmas in India?" I asked.

"When I first began to work in the zenänas," said my aunt, who was a missionary, "we had no Christmases. But things are changed now, or you would not be suspiciously watching the monkey here in the very court of a zenäna. Men, especially strangers, seldom used to be allowed to enter a zenäna, and the women as seldom went outside of it and its court except for the purpose of worship."

A zenäna in India, I should here explain, is the part of the house assigned to the women and children. In former times it was really a beautiful prison for women and girls. Beautiful it may well have been made, for before the English rule in India the women of India were little better than slaves, and the zenänas were nearly all that they saw of life. It is one of the purposes of the women's missionary societies of England and the United States, to educate the women and to secure for them a better life. This had been my aunt's work for a number of years.

The house which she had rented and its zenäna were as open to strangers as any English home. It was full of girls and Bible women under instruction, and of medical supplies. The latter fact may seem strange, but my aunt had received a medical education as a part of her preparation for her work.

I had had a long talk with aunt, had told her the news from her friends at home, and she had given me a view of her life and work, and then we had gone out into the court to enjoy the cooler air. I had laid my guide-book, which had a red cover and which folded like a large pocket-book, on a bamboo seat, and had interested myself in the showers of blossoms, the peacock, and the solemn and inquisitive looking monkey. My attention was diverted by the entrance of an old woman. I was surprised to find that, though an Indian woman, she could speak English well, and was told by my aunt that it was on this account she had taken her into her service some years before, and had retained her. Her girlhood had been passed in an English family.

"She is a faithful old creature," said my aunt. — "Just look at that monkey!"

This was an unexpected turn in the conversation. I looked. The monkey was solemnly seated on the wall as before, but had my guide-book in one hand and was holding my spectacles across its eyes with the other.

I was about to say "Shoo!" or "Scat!" I was not sure as to what would be the proper term in which to speak to a monkey, when in a twinkling he disappeared, — guide-book, spectacles, and all.

"He thought it was a hymn-book," said the old Indian woman.

"Surely," said I, "monkeys in India do not sing! Your work has not gone so far as that!"

"No," said my aunt; "but nothing pleases him more than to sit on the wall with a hymn-book in his hand, just as he has seen us hold the book in meetings. He seems to think that a book makes him more like folks."

"WE HAD GONE OUT INTO THE COURT TO ENJOY THE COOLER AIR."

"But my spectacles! how did he ever get them? I put them in my vest-pocket, and did not miss them."

"But you just passed under the cocoanut-palm with your glasses loose in your pocket."

"Aunt," said I, "I think that monkey needs some further moral instruction."

"I will get your book and spectacles again," said the old woman, kindly. And she left the house and soon returned with them, after which the monkey came again and sat down solemnly beside the peacock on the wall.

"Oh, you villain!" said I.

He made a face at me.

I stamped.

He made another hideous grimace.

"I would not plague him," said the old woman, gently. "It is better, I think, to have the good-will of a monkey than his ill-will. You will find him a very pleasant friend."

There was something very kind in the old woman's reproof and spirit; so I changed my expression of face toward my new friend the monkey, and he changed his at once toward me, just like a face in a mirror. Then I laughed, and he jabbered.

Then the queerest Christmas eve that I have ever known followed this introductory episode. We sat down in the court, — my aunt, the old woman, and myself, — with my friend the monkey on the wall. Then some zenäna girls joined us, and afterward an American missionary with her two little girls.

We talked of the day in America, — of the bells, the green churches amid the snow, and of the fabulous Santa Claus.

"You have no Santa Claus in India," said I to Aunt. "It must be a great economy."

"But we have the Mysterious Fakir here," said Aunt. "I like him better than Santa Claus. He is one of the most interesting beings of whom I ever heard. He brings good luck."

"Is he the rolling fakir?" asked one of the little girls.

"The rolling fakir?" asked I. "What is that?"

"Oh," said my aunt, "there is an order of fakirs in India that roll."

"Where?"

"In the road."

"How far?"

"Well, often a hundred miles."

"A hundred miles! How?"

"Over and over."

"Roll over and over a hundred miles! What becomes of their clothes?"

"Fakirs have but very scanty clothing; only a strip of cloth."

"Does n't it kill them?"

"Oh, no."

"Roll over and over a hundred miles in the road!" I laughed.

The monkey gibbered. I felt in all my pockets to see if anything were gone.

"Well! well!" said I; "India is a queer country. Tell us about the Mysterious Fakir."

"An old nurse first told me the story some years ago. I have since met this mysterious man several times."

"Are there many fakirs in India?" I asked.

"Yes, there are — or there used to be — several million."

"Do they all roll?" I asked.

"Oh, no. Some perform their religious vows by hanging upon trees with their heads downward; some sit with uplifted arms; but most of them beg. I once saw a fakir who had sat upon a rock, almost naked, exposed to the sun, for years, until his skin was tanned like leather. He looked like an image, and seemed utterly lost to the world; and the people used to worship him daily as though he were an idol."

"But tell me more about the rolling fakir," I asked. "I should think that the wild beasts would kill him, in a journey of a hundred miles, — that the tigers would find him and eat him."

"It seems strange, but I have never heard of any fakirs being killed by a tiger. But your thought brings to mind an adventure that I once met in travelling through a jungle, and the very jungle through which the fakir of whom I have spoken often makes his journeys. I will tell you this story, which will be very oddly different from those which our English and American friends are telling in our old homes: —

"I was travelling one hot summer day in the open country with a party of natives, when I saw in the highway a dark object rolling over and over, which looked like an enormous serpent. The natives saw it at the same time, and appeared greatly pleased. 'The fakir! the fakir!' they exclaimed. Now, it is considered a very fortunate thing to meet this mysterious man, and it is supposed to bring good luck to follow him.

"The natives hurried me on until we came to the fakir, when we travelled very slowly behind him.

"He did not seem to heed us, but to be wholly absorbed in what he held to be his religious duty. He had black eyes which seemed fixed, and dark hair which was filled with dust; and he was quite naked, except a breechcloth.

"We came to a jungle, and I was glad to feel the cool shadows of trees. At last the jungle grew dense, and the way became very narrow.

"I was very much interested in the movement of the fakir as he rolled over and over, and my eye followed him until my head grew dizzy.

"Suddenly a shadow seemed to darken the narrow way. I looked up, and directly before us saw an enormous elephant. I was frightened and confused. The jungle was so dense that I could not see how I was to get out of the way; and what was to become of the poor rolling fakir?

"The natives did not seem to feel or express any alarm.

"I stopped in amazement when I discovered that behind this large elephant was a smaller one; and I soon found that these two were not all, — there was a troop of elephants in the narrow way, following each other in single file, guided by a mahout.

"I turned to run back.

"'It is all right! all right!' exclaimed the natives in chorus. 'Come on!'

"'All right!' I exclaimed. 'How are we to pass the elephants?'

"'Come on! come on! It is all right!' exclaimed the natives again.

"Had I gone mad? All right, and a troop of elephants travelling toward us in the narrow way, and the jungle an almost solid grove on either side!

"'But the fakir?' I said, still retreating.

"'All right! it is all right! The elephants know! it is all right!'

"I expected now to see the elephants stop. It surely could not be all right for them to trample over the body of the rolling fakir. Would they stop and let him roll under them, and let us pass under them or around them?

"No; they came directly on, like an enormous moving mass of machinery.

"The great elephant had now reached the fakir. He put out his trunk, and, to my astonishment, lifted the fakir to his head. Then he dropped his hind legs under his own body slowly until he looked like a hill, and the pious fakir rolled down his back.

"The second elephant did the same, and the fakir was passed on in this way over the whole troop of elephants.

"Then one of the natives led me up to the first elephant. I found myself suddenly lifted into the air. I then felt the elephant's body settling down. I rose up on the elephant's neck, and looked down the huge creature's back. It was an inclined plane, except that the muscles were humped like a flight of stairs. I walked down cautiously and very slowly.

"I was then passed over the whole troop, as were the natives, and we were all soon following the rolling fakir through the jungle.

"'You will have good luck,' said the natives, as we came in a few hours to a bamboo town.

"'Why?' I asked.

"'Because you met the fakir.'"

So passed my Christmas eve in a zenäna, and I have never forgotten the odd scenes and the odd story. I afterward learned that in the narrow streets of certain Indian towns trained elephants pass people over their backs in this remarkable way.

The evening became cool and delicious. The stars shone brightly through

"THE PIOUS FAKIR ROLLED DOWN HIS BACK."

the dusk, and the breath of flowers floated on the cooling air. The old Indian woman sang a hymn in the native tongue. Then I said "Good-night" to my friends, but had almost forgotten the monkey. I recalled him, turned, and made a grimace to him; he made a face to me, several of them in fact, but all expressive of much friendliness and good-will. And, thinking of all my experiences in this strange part of the world, I fell asleep on a divan, and for the first Christmas night in my life not to be awakened by the ringing of joyful bells or the singing of sweet carols.

THE STORY OF THE RACHASSEE.

The Rachassee is found among the national emblems of Siam, especially on temples. He was a fabulous monster, and though not a bear came of the bear family. He grew to monstrous size, and became the King of beasts.

The first King of the animal kingdom, according to the Siamese, was an owl; and a very wise King he must have been. The second was a crow; and he not unlikely looked well to the affairs of his kingdom. The third was a pheasant, — a very royal-looking bird, — and the last was a peacock.

But the peacock was proud, and the animals rebelled, and a very democratic assembly was called to elect a King. The elephant had the most votes and was chosen, but the tiger would not submit to him. There was anarchy. At this time came forward the Rachassee, a bear-lion of great courage and power. He offered himself as a champion. He fought all the other great beasts and overcame them. He then began to rule, and chose a mountain top for his throne.

He made one very wise law for the beasts. It was: Never go near mankind. But the elephant and horse disobeyed the law, and are suffering punishment for it to this day.

He reigned for a time in great dignity; but the dog became jealous of his power, and determined to destroy him.

"There is," said the dog, "another King in the mountains as powerful as yourself."

"Show him to me!" said the Rachassee.

"Come with me!" said the dog.

The dog led him to the top of a cleft mountain, between whose precipices was a clear lake, like a great mirror.

"Look down!" said the dog.

The Rachassee looked down and saw his own image in the lake, and thought that it was another and a rival forest King. He shook his head in defiance; so did the beast below.

The Rachassee could not endure this, and leaped over the precipice and

"A VERY WISE KING HE MUST HAVE BEEN"

was killed. He had, however, made princes of the white elephants, and they succeeded him and still rule.

Relics of the Rachassee were long sought for, and those who obtained them became lords and princes.

"THE IMAGES OF THE RACHASSEE AND THE ELEPHANT ARE USUALLY PLACED ON THE OUTSIDE OF THE TEMPLES."

After a time the Rachassee was born again; and as he had developed great courage as a beast, he was born this time above the estate of men, as a god. So people came to worship him.

This was before the days of Buddha; and so the images of the Rachassee and the Elephant are usually placed on the outside of the temples, to indicate the more ancient worship.

He still roars at times in the deep forests. His voice is like thunder, and it splits the drums of the ears of those who hear it. I never heard of a Siamese, however, whose ears were thus split.

Ivory admirably acted the part of the Astrologer from Siam, and entertained the company afterward by a medley of odd and curious riddles and puzzles. One of these, he said, would not be a puzzle in any other language but our own, so it was a double puzzle. It was this: —

"A blind fiddler had a sister, but the blind fiddler's sister had no brother."

Some grammatical sentences which he gave us to parse were as curious: —

"His office *as judge* is desirable."
"*The more* I look at it *the brighter* it appears."
"I was not aware of his *being* an *officer*."
"*To be* or not *to be*, is the *question*."
"And Harry's *flesh* it fell away."
"*Two times two* are *four*."

And the following in the same vein is as odd: —

"We are little airy creatures,
All of different voice and features:
One of us in glass is set,
One of us you 'll find in jet;
The other you may see in tin,
And the fourth a box within ;
If the fifth you should pursue,
It can never fly from you."

Among other things that Ivory proposed during the family festival was the forming of a Band of Mercy. He could not live without a mission. His plan was to organize a society at the hotel, unite it to the Boston Society, and then to multiply it among the negroes.

My aunt Marden sympathized with him in the proposed movement, and ended the Christmas entertainment with an odd story, that not only pleased Ivory, but quite delighted us all.

MY FIRST CHRISTMAS OFFERING.

"Somebody has got to drop that kitten," said my aunt to me one day, when I was a little girl.

"Why?" I asked innocently. I was a little girl of ten years. I had been left an orphan, and had been given a home with my aunt in a simple country town.

"*Why?* Do you think that I am goin' to raisin' cats for a livin'? We've got two already, and I'm not goin' to raise any more. I'll tie it up in a little bean-basket, and when you go to the Children's Offerin', you just drop it down the old well by the brier pastur', and that will be the end of that."

"Oh, Aunt!" exclaimed I, in horror.

"What now? Nobody ever draws any water out of that well only for the cattle in the summer-time. It won't hurt it a mite."

"But 't will hurt the little kitten."

"The kitten won't know anything about it. It's only just got its eyes open."

"But —"

"But what?"

"Wouldn't it be wrong?"

"It is wrong to drop kittens round at other folks' doors, as some folks do. But 't is our own well."

The wee kitten lay in my lap. It was about three weeks old, and oh, how cunning it looked! — a little ball of yellow and white, with bright eyes and the faintest possible mew.

A yellow kitten was not common, and I beheld it with delight when its fond mother first brought it into the sitting-room in her mouth. The old cat and I were great friends, and she showed great pride when she laid down on the rug before me this little yellow kitten. I had adopted the bit of velvety beauty at once, and had dreamed that we would be playmates when the summer came.

"ITS FOND MOTHER FIRST BROUGHT IT INTO THE SITTING-ROOM IN HER MOUTH."

Drop the kitten down in the well! I could almost as soon have dropped a little baby into such an awful receptacle. I was an obedient child, and a truthful one, but I at once resolved in my heart that I would never do a dreadful deed like that, and began to devise in my mind ways of saving my pet. I sat in silence, thinking of the cold well, the ice, and the bean-basket, and wondering how it could have entered my aunt's heart to plan such a tragedy.

"Come, Mattie, you've tended that kitten long enough. There's somethin' to do in this world besides waitin' upon cats. Have you got your lesson for the doin's this afternoon?"

"What lesson, aunt?"

"Why, have n't I told you over and over again, and here you are studyin' cats, like a regular stupid! 'What lesson?' Don't you know that the rector said that when you made your offerin' you must repeat a verse of poetry, or passage of Scriptur', or somethin' or other? Now, what are you goin' to say?"

"I don't know, Aunt."

"No, you're not goin' to say, 'I don't know, Aunt'; that's nothin' to say. You're goin' to say somethin' about charity, or mercy, or —"

"She might say, 'A merciful man is merciful to his beast,'" said Uncle, looking up from his almanac. "How would that do?"

"It would n't do at all. Say, Mattie, 'Blessed are the merciful.'"

The beautiful words added to my horror. I had a very tender conscience, and my mother had taught it to respond to all such teachings as this. I thought of her now, and began to cry. Aunt was busy at the stove, changing the pots and kettles. Suddenly she turned to me and said, —

"What is it?"

I repeated the text.

"That's right, Mattie; that shows your bringin' up. Now, I have made a beautiful calico apron, and put it into a box; so when your name is called, you just take the box and go up to the pulpit and drop the box into the basket, just as you see the rest of 'em do, and say these words. And it is time for you to be gettin' ready, and I'll get the kitten ready. Here, let me have it."

I shall never forget that afternoon as I started out on my double commission. It was the day before Christmas. The country was white with snow, and the long pine woods were bright with crystals. The roads were gay with sleigh-bells, and the ponds were merry with the voices of the skaters. I should have been wonderfully happy had it not been for the little basket on my arm and its precious contents.

My aunt followed me to the gate. So did the old cat. Her eyes were filled with reproach.

"Now, what are you goin' to say, Mattie?"

"'A merciful man is —'"

"No, no; that's not what you are to say. There ain't no truth in that, anyhow; that's one of Ben Franklin's proverbs, or some such worldly-minded poet. What you are to say is this;" and she gave me my lesson again with emphasis. "Now, don't you forget. What a beautiful walk you will have! I wish I was goin' too. I always loved to do good to the poor."

The old cat purred around me and rubbed herself against my feet, as though she too had a parting word to say. I was in full sympathy with her. "Mew!" How it went to my heart! She knew that her kitten was in the basket, and that her family had from time to time mysteriously disappeared. She seemed to have confidence in me, but to be very uncertain in regard to what was going to happen. "Mew!"

My aunt seized the cat and took her into the house, saying, as she shut the door, " Don't forget to take the kitten, Mattie."

I was not likely to forget the kitten. The bit of a basket on my wrist already seemed as heavy as a basket of grain. I started toward the church. What was I to do? My first impulse was to drop the kitten at some door as I passed along, but I recalled what my aunt said about the meanness of such an act as that. I opened the basket and peeped in. There came from it a little faint, helpless "Mew!" just like a whisper. I opened the basket further. Oh, how cunning the little thing looked! I thought of the old cat and her family affliction. I came to the well by the pasture wall. I could go no further. My feelings quite overcame me, and in spite of the cold, I sat down on an icy stepping-stone in the stone wall near the well, and began to cry.

"What is the matter with my little girl?"

The voice was very kind and pleasant. I looked up. It was the rector. I was dumb. What could I say?

"You surely ought to be very happy, my little girl, with *two* offerings for the poor on such a day as this. Give me your box, my little girl, and let me take your hand, and we will walk along together."

Was ever a child before placed in such a situation as this? "*Two* offerings!" The words brought to my darkened mind an idea. I would put *both* my offerings into the contribution basket, and would say over them, as I dropped them in, the words of the "worldly-minded poet," for my lips could never use Scripture in such a complicated moral situation. I felt relieved, and was proud of the rector's attention and company.

We reached the chapel. It was hung with evergreens, and in front of the pulpit was an immense basket, also trimmed with evergreens, and partly

"HER EYES WERE FILLED WITH REPROACH."

surrounded with pot plants. Into this, at the proper time, the children were to drop their offerings, and repeat while they did so the world's best thoughts on charity.

The rector had planned this service, and it had been a part of the yearly festival for a long time. The offerings consisted largely of home-made articles, and these were given on Christmas morning to the poor women and children of the parish.

"It educates the children to be charitable," said the good rector. "Children should be as much educated to be feeling and benevolent as to be industrious. What a child is before he is ten, he will be all his life. It is not only for the present that I do this thing; these charities are only the seed: they will blossom when I am gone."

Dear old man! He has long been gone, and the seeds still blossom.

The children sang their carols. Then came the literary exercises and offerings. My name was called. I walked up to the basket with trembling limbs and made my *two* offerings, and said, with a gasp, "A merciful man is merciful to his beast." I saw a look of surprise in the old rector's face as I made this unexpected announcement; but it went away, and gave place to the usual benevolent smile.

I was not happy after I returned to my seat. My feet were in perpetual motion. It seemed to relieve my palpitating heart to swing them like two pendulums. During the last prayer I chanced to kick over a footstool in the pew in the excitement of my nervous motions. It was very still in the room at the time, and the *bang* was most startling. I then felt more excited than ever. I was covered with perspiration, and I could hear my heart beat.

"SHE 'S BROUGHT IT HOME, BASKET AND ALL."

I dreaded the question, when I should return, "Did you drop the kitten?" What should I say?

Uncle had "chills" when I returned. Aunt was giving him a "sweat," and she only said to me, "Did you have a good time, Mattie?"

Christmas morning came. It had been many times a happy hour to me, the early light of the day of the world's festival. But I had passed a feverish night, and Aunt never acted the pleasant fiction of Santa Claus, as my poor mother had done.

I did not rise early. I heard the distant bells ring, and thought of my old home. Then I heard a pitiful cry at the front door: "Mew!"

It was repeated over and over. At last I heard my aunt go to the door. She closed it with a bang, and cried, —

"Mattie! Mattie! get up! I shall give it up now. Oh, merciful me!"

"What, Aunt? What has happened?"

"You come right down and see. That cat has been and gone and got her kitten right out of the well."

"Is it dead?" I asked tremblingly.

"Dead? no; just as alive as it was when I put it into the basket. She's brought it home, basket and all."

"Give it to me, Aunt, for a Christmas present. I'll be real good for the whole year, and wash the dishes every morning."

"Well, I will, Mattie, since your heart is set upon it; and it is all so mysterious. This is a queer, queer world."

I was very helpful that day. I wondered how it all could have happened, but I never said a word. Somehow the cat must have got into the chapel and taken the kitten out of the basket, as the presents were to remain in the basket during the night. A few months later I relieved my unhappy conscience by making a full confession to my aunt and to the good old rector.

So ended our Christmas with Ivory.

Quarrels arose among the young negroes, and Ivory always acted as a peacemaker. While thus acting one day, a negro boy violently kicked him, and, a hemorrhage following, a physician had to be called.

"Did you knock the young scamp over?" asked the latter.

"No; he was sorry a moment after, and that made me sorry for him," said Ivory.

After the doctor had gone, he said to me, "Tell little Pomp that the hurt is not serious, and I shall be better soon."

I was indignant. "Ivory," I said, "you have no spirit at all. If you allow such habits of cowardice to grow, where will it end?"

"Oh, Manton, if I am ever called to face danger for duty's sake,

"A NEGRO BOY VIOLENTLY KICKED HIM."

you will not find me a coward. I sometimes think I may be called to give my life for some good cause; if so, the cause may have it. I cannot be cruel. I cannot do wrong, but I can suffer wrong. Some day you will have cause to change your opinion of me."

It was a prophecy. I recall it now with a tender heart. It is the "loving who are the daring," and the sympathetic who have the most to offer to others when the day of testing comes. Poor Ivory! it was his last Christmas. How beautiful was the memory that he left, in view of the events that followed!

CHAPTER X.

JAVA. — THE STORY OF THE FLYING DUTCHWOMAN.

N March, Ivory received a letter from his father which was a surprise to me.

BANGKOK, SIAM.

MY DEAR SON, — The East India Company for the running of telegraph lines have new plans for Sumatra, Java, and the Malay Peninsula. I do not know definitely what these plans are, but they wish to employ new telegraph-operators and linemen, and I am asked to recommend some English and American young men to them, to whom they may apply. If you will now return to their service, your pay will be advanced on account of your experience. They desire to employ you again, and wish me to say this to you.

Would your cousin Manton like a place in this service? If so, I could secure it for him, as a practical telegraph-operator or as a lineman, or both. He has had experience as a telegrapher in the great hotels, and he would receive very liberal payment for service in the Company. His expenses would be paid to and from Bangkok, and his salary would not be less than £400 for the first year.

The rest of the letter was personal.

Had a title and a fortune fallen to me, I could not have been more astonished.

"You will go?" said Ivory.

"Will you return?"

"Yes; I like the service."

A JAVAN BASKET-MERCHANT.

"And the Company like you."

"I tried to serve them well."

"But I have not studied telegraphy as I ought, to become a lineman."

"Take up the study now. The mere running of lines is easily learned; you know the rest, except the recent electrical experiments and improvements. Get the latest books on the subject, and we will study them together."

I hardly slept for a week. My friends in Florida advised me to accept the situation offered, and to go to Bangkok with Ivory. I considered the matter well, and decided to go. I had never dreamed of an employment in life like that, or in such a part of the world.

Another letter came to Ivory from his father soon. One of the new plans of the country was work in Java.

Java? I knew little of the island. My only knowledge of it was derived from the school Geography, the "Old Government Coffee" that we had used at the hotel, and a very queer old coast story that I had heard when spending a winter in a town near Cape Ann.

It was a long time since I had heard the quaint old story which had pictured to me Java. I recalled it now, and told it to Ivory one day, and afterward to the people of the hotel at a "coffee party" in which Java coffee was the principal beverage.

THE FLYING DUTCHWOMAN.

I remember her well. She lived in a house, or rather hut, roofed with kelp, and in the summer covered with morning-glories. She was short and stout, and her hair was gray, and she did not look as though she could *fly*.

But the fishermen said that the old Dutchwoman had wings. They had often seen a dark mysterious object passing through the air at night, along the coast; and whenever any such indefinable form was seen in the starlight, the simple people claimed that it was the Flying Dutchwoman. It was one of the awe-inspiring events of the village, to hear some new tale of the shadowy flight of the lone Dutchwoman at night, among the bats and owls, the night-hawks and night-herons. One old sailor declared that he had seen her "flying right into the stars;" but it will be hard to believe, in this scientific age, that she ever ascended quite as high as *that*.

"SHE DID NOT LOOK AS THOUGH SHE COULD FLY."

How did the idea form in the minds of the villagers that the harmless old lady could fly? The evolution of the story, like that of the German popular legend of Dr. Faustus or Faust, was a very simple one. A half-century before she had come to the village, the witchcraft delusion had more or less excited all the villages along the coast, and in many towns there were shattered old women who were believed to be able to fly. The reason for these aerial journeys was supposed to be a nightly gathering of witches in some mysterious retreat in the forest. There, in an unknown forest circle, the old women thus provided with wings were fancied to gather to meet the Evil One and to *dance*. The popular fancy pictured them as dancing in a circle under the light of the moon, and sometimes as surrounded by cats and owls.

In several instances poor old women were put to death for being accused of attending these awful and mysterious gatherings. Cotton Mather was the leading clergyman in New England at that time, and he led what he believed to be a holy warfare against witches and "powers of darkness;" and under the influence of his opinions, even a brother clergyman had been put to death as being a *wizard*. The people believed all the marvellous stories that he told in his "Magnalia" and "New English Canaan," and followed his teachings as though he had been an inspired prophet.

The witchcraft delusion passed away in a measure, but it left its influence on the minds of the people for an hundred years. Queer people were no longer brought before the courts as witches, but they were still suspected of witchcraft, and so became a terror to themselves and the community.

While this superstition still lingered, Hans Hollander, a young trader, afterward a fisherman, and his pleasant wife Mary, came to the fishing-

THE JAVA COFFEE-MARKET.

village and built them a house or hut near the coast, on the borders of the town.

Hans was employed by the Netherlands Trading Company, which controlled the trade of Java, as their agent in bringing Java, or Old Government, coffee to the port of Boston. This company was formed by King William I. in 1824, and in the next fifty years so developed Java as to make the island a mine of riches to the Dutch. It lends money to young coffee and sugar growers, transports the products of Java to Amsterdam, and thence to the markets of the world.

The Dutch ships used to remain in the port of Boston from January until mild weather, engaged in trade; and Hans came to like America, and bought a little place that had once been occupied by one of his own countrymen on the coast. The house was a very simple one, but he and his wife lived happily; she spending the summers alone, and he the winters in part with her.

"THE FISHERMEN SAID SHE HAD WINGS."

The Hollanders were social folk, and very hospitable on small means; people used to go to see them on long winter evenings to drink Java coffee, and to hear Hans relate the wonders of Java. He used to tell stories about the swallows' nests of Java, and the adventures of those who gathered them for the Chinese markets; of the caverns at Karang Bollong, in Java, with their hundreds of thousands of swallows, which yielded to the markets a half-million of nests.

Among Hans's wonderful stories was that of Boro Buddor, or of Great Buddha, the ruins of which he himself had seen in Java. Buddhism was the old religion of Java, but was overthrown by Mohammedanism. Boro Buddor was the great Buddhist temple of Java. It was a pyramid as large as a hill, with terraces filled with most beautiful statues. It was, in its day, one of the most beautiful structures in the world.

Hans died at Java; but his wife continued to live on Cape Ann, a lonely woman. She supported herself by hard work among the families of the place.

The story of the "Flying Dutchman" — a ship that was supposed to be doomed forever to sail the sea and never come to port — was a favorite story of the old Amsterdam sailors who traded among the islands of the Indian Ocean and brought coffee from Java to Amsterdam, and was one of the wonder-tales among the Cape Ann fishermen as well at this time. Mary Hollander herself used to tell it to the children after her hard day's work at the wash-tub, although she did not pretend that it was true.

Around the cottage were several martin-bird cages on high poles. Hans had made them and set them up, and he used to call the martin-birds Java swallows. After his death his wife had planted hop-vines around them; and she always seemed glad, I have been told, when the swallows returned, because the return of the birds recalled her happy life with Hans.

Mary grew old and odd. She kept a black cat, which was regarded as a suspicious circumstance in those days. The great woods at the back of the town were filled with birds — "quarks" they were called in the local tongue — that came to the coast at night for shell-fish. These birds were dark, with long necks. They flew in small flocks; and in the dusk or in the starlight or moonlight the flocks appeared like one body. These flocks of "quarks" often settled down on the coast at low tide, just outside the village, near Mary Hollander's simple hut; and here the local sportsmen sought them, and we do not doubt that it was the return flight of these birds laden with food for their young that gave the impression of poor Mary Hollander's journeys among the bats and herons and "into the stars." Certain it is that she became known as the "Flying Dutchwoman;" and many people, and young

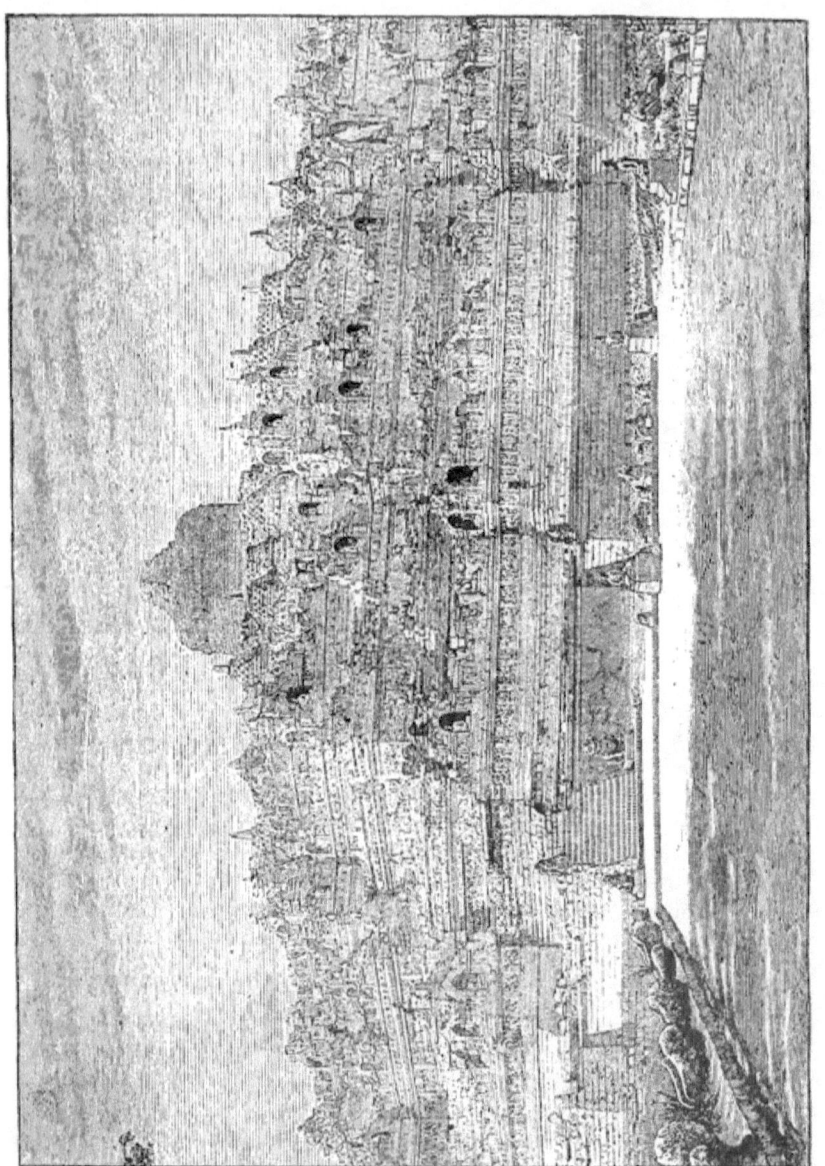

THE GREAT BUDDHIST TEMPLE OF JAVA.

people especially, shunned the vicinity of her hut at night; and awful stories about her multiplied as the poor old woman grew, in a measure, helpless with years.

Peter Skillet was a young fisherman whose life had been largely passed on the sea. He had heard the story of the "Flying Dutchman," and believed it, and was afraid lest that airy craft with "shivered" sails should appear off the Banks. He had also heard all of the many tales about the "Flying Dutchwoman," and believed them all. In fact, he himself said that he had seen, when lying off the coast in his fishing-smack, a dark object rise from the door of Mary Hollander's hut, and soar toward the moon. He thought it not unlikely that old Mary "had a hut in the moon also."

The years went on. The old woman covered her roof with sea-weed anew every fall; and the springs brought back the "quarks" to the woods, and the summers the morning-glories to the old dame's windows and doors. And Peter Skillet became of age; and one summer, while in port, he placed his affections on a thrifty farmer's daughter, named Molly Smart.

It seemed a fitting choice; but the courtship from the first involved a courage and daring as great as ancient knighthood. Molly lived about half a mile from the Flying Dutchwoman's hut, and the road from the village passed her very door.

In the daytime the road seemed safe to travel; but at night one was likely to meet Mary Hollander's *cat*. In fact, one young fisherman had actually seen that black cat running along the fence in the moonlight; and although he would have perilled his life in a storm or tempest at sea, his nerves could not stand such a shock as *that*, and he had turned around with wild eyes, and fled to the safe walls of home to await the morning light for the renewal of his journey.

Another young fisherman had seen the cat on the beach while he was digging clams. He had dropped his clam-hoe at once, and he left to that dark and mysterious animal the results of his labor during the tide.

It may seem quite improbable that men who yearly dared the perils of the Banks, and whose occupation demanded the highest courage, should run from a *cat;* but it was so. The village was full of people who often faced death at sea, and shrank not from the most appalling actual dangers, and yet who could not have been hired to pass poor Mary Hollander's hut at night. No terror can equal superstitious fear.

Soon after Peter Skillet's affections became centred on Molly Smart, he grew melancholy.

"What's the matter, Peter?" asked his mother one day. "There did n't used to be a more chipper lad in all the town, and now there is n't one that is more dumpish. What ails ye? Come now, Peter, tell me all; sure you have n't a better friend in all the world than your old mother."

"You know, mother — Mary," said Peter, cautiously.

"Handsome Mary Smart? Molly?"

"Yes, mother."

"Well, you never heard me say anything ag'in Molly, did ye?"

"No, but goin' to see her — you know, the witch and the *air*, and the — you can't tell what's going to happen."

"There's no danger in the daytime, Peter. Go on Sunday to see Molly; no, that would n't be quite the thing, to do your courtin' on Sunday. Go across lots, Peter, nights."

"But — "

"But what, Peter?"

"The cat."

"Pooh on the cat! You would n't see the cat if you went across lots. 'T would be an awful bad sign, I 'll allow. But this world is full of terrible things, and you must take your chances. Yes, Peter, you 'll have to go across lots. I don't see any other way."

"But Solomon Graves saw that cat one night way off in the huckleberry pasture. You know old Solomon Graves. A week after that he had a fit, and did n't live twenty-four hours. And then when *she flies*, she goes *that* way."

"I should hate to see her, Peter. I declare I should."

"I should, too," said Peter, most truthfully. "I should *scrooch* right down like a chicken before a hawk. I do believe that my heart would give one bump, and I would drop right down dead. I do think that there should be some law ag'in people like old Mary Hollander. Cotton Mather was right; and people in this day are too wise for their own good. Such people ought to be hung."

"Be careful, Peter; be careful."

Peter turned pale. "Now I have said it, have n't I, mother? You don't suppose that *she* knows, do you, and that she will cast an evil eye on me for it? Now I shall be more frightened than ever."

"But educated people now say, Peter, that there are no such things as ghosts, and witches, and evil eyes, and the like; that such things are nothing but imagination."

"Then what did you tell me such stories for when I was a boy? Ain't I called the boldest boy in the fishing-fleet? I never trembled before anything in my life but haunts, just those haunts. I never trembled upon the mast; but

"HERE THE LOCAL SPORTSMEN SOUGHT THEM."

after your stories of haunted graveyards, and witches, and evil spells, and people sellin' their souls to the Old Boy, and what not, I've made the bed just tremble many a night. There ought to be a law ag'in such things; and if there are no such things, there ought to be a law ag'in teachin' boys and girls that there *are* such things."

"You talk like a philosopher, Peter, but there is no human law that can have any effect on the doin's of the spirit world. But, Peter, I have another plan. Go on horseback! You could then scoot by like magic, — just like a flying horseman."

A sudden light came into Peter's face.

"You are a foresighted woman, mother. I'll have to ride fast, but I will do it."

Peter had a pony, only broken to the saddle, that went like the wind. Twice a week, early in the evening, he mounted this pony and rode slowly with a drawn rein over to Molly Smart's. His return was as precipitate as his going had been deliberate. He would throw both arms around the pony's neck, give the little animal a cut, and would be borne back to the village as on the enchanted steed of Arabian fiction, or as though he were riding the wind. He never saw the cat in these late hours; and if that dread animal had seen him, she would surely have suddenly disappeared.

Nor did he ever see the old woman in the air. He did sometimes see a light in the window of the hut in the distance, but he never would look that way more than once on the flying journey. Courting with the pony now seemed to be a perfect success. He gained great local credit by it, too.

"There is a young man," said the fishermen, proudly, "who never feared the face of day, nor a storm, nor any other thing. The powers of darkness could never turn *him* from his purpose. There is a young man for the port to honor!"

The port became so proud of Peter, that, when the militia met in the autumn after these bold rides, he was elected Captain of the Coast Guards. He was soon afterward honored again by being elected pound-keeper by the town. The pound was situated just *this* side of Dame Hollander's hut, — a very undesirable locality to most aspirants for the office.

"You owe it all to your mother, Peter," said Mrs. Skillet. "'T is I and the pony, Peter, that deserves all the credit. But go on; maybe it will come out all right. It will if *you* don't get scared; but there's never no tellin' what may happen."

Molly Smart was greatly esteemed in the community, but there existed one prejudice against her. Her mother was an "Episcopal," and Molly had also followed the Prayer-book. The village was strictly Puritan, and held the Church of England in much disfavor at the time, although to-day the Episcopal Chapel is its principal place of worship.

Peter and Molly had a charming summer's courtship. Peter was looked upon as the Flying Horseman, and as more than a match for the Flying Dutchwoman; and a kind of romance gathered around him, despite his homely name.

Molly desired to be married on Christmas eve. It required some further courage on the part of Peter to consent to this.

"What for do you want to be married at that time? It seems to me kinder like Popery; and they do say that *she* wanders about the earth and air on that night without any head on, and casts an evil eye."

This was the local tradition. Just how an old lady without a "head on" could cast an evil eye, was not easy to be explained; but that old Mary Hollander wandered about the beach about Christmas time gathering pieces of wreckage for fuel, was true; and also that she did this with a shawl over her head. It was also usually quite sickly in the town about Christmas time, and all epidemic sickness for years was attributed to the Flying Dutchwoman and her evil eye.

"If we should meet her, Molly, on our weddin' night, too, and she should scare the horse, it would be *awful*, after all I 've 'dured for ye, too."

But Molly had a strong desire for a Christmas wedding. It would be like the fine old English days of which her mother had told her. An Episcopal Justice of the Peace lived in the adjoining town, and it was arranged that the couple should go to him early on Christmas eve and be married, and then return and receive the congratulations of a wedding party who should assemble at the bride's home. The mother of the bride had some means of her own, and was ambitious that this wedding party should be very generous, gay, and hospitable.

Peter thought that he had really grown bold during his courtship. He had passed the hut of the Flying Dutchwoman fifty times, and often late at night, and received no harm. He had also grown proud of his reputation for temerity. The town had praised and honored him; and now came into his heart a plan for celebrating his own marriage by an act of heroism which, like Captain Miles Standish's exploit at Merry Mount, should make his name truly historic.

"What is the use of bein' under the bondage of fear any longer, as the parson says? I 'm just goin' to relieve the town of its terror, and then I 'll be here, I do declare I will. After the weddin' I 'll just take some of the militia and go and tear down the hut of the Flying Dutchwoman, and make her go to the poorhouse."

"HE HAD TURNED AROUND WITH WILD EYES, AND FLED."

He unfolded his new and daring plan to the boldest members of the military company, but they did not seem eager to volunteer.

"This fightin' men is one thing, but goin' to war with the powers of the air is another," said one. But nevertheless Peter found several young men who promised to follow him, unless he should "be carried off bodily," in which case they were quite willing to be left behind.

New suspicions against the poor old woman seemed to make the bold experiment very desirable and commendable. Some fishers during their last trip to the Banks had seen a dark object one night in the air, and the expedition had proved unlucky and a part of the craft had been lost. It was whispered darkly that the Flying Dutchwoman had caused the disaster.

Again, poultry had disappeared at night from the farmyards. From the manner of the disappearance it was conjectured that the prey had been taken into the air. A man who had lost several fine fowls had heard them *squalling* in the sky. The superstitious were sure that they had been carried away by the Flying Dutchwoman. In fact, all the disasters and whatever was mysterious in the village came to be attributed to the Flying Dutchwoman.

But old Mary Hollander had her friends, — people who knew her private worth and innocence, and the cruelty of the popular superstition.

Mary Hollander's people had been Catholics, and she had brought with her many innocent customs from over the sea that were disliked in the little port. She had a great reverence for Christmas, and she was supposed to be particularly busy in travelling along the coast and in the air about the time of the English and Latin holidays.

There was a ballad that she used to sing to the children about Christmas time, before she was so universally shunned, that was at one time regarded as very curious and harmless, but finally as the work of the dark agencies with which she was supposed to deal. It certainly was a very strange composition, and the music was as mournful as the words. It came to be repeated by the old women and children with a kind of superstitious terror.

> "This ae night, this ae night,
>   Every night and a',
> Fire and sleet and candle-light,
>   And may Christ save thy soul!
>
> "When thou from the world shall pass,
>   Every night and a',
> To Winney Muir thou 'll come at last,
>   And may Christ save thy soul!

"If thou hast given housen and shoon,
    Every night and a',
Sit thee down and put them on,
    And may Christ save thy soul!

"If housen and shoon thou hast given nane,
    Every night and a',
The winnies will prick thee to the bare bane,
    And may Christ save thy soul!

"From Winney Muir when thou art past.
    Every night and a',
To Brigg o' Doom thou 'll come at last,
    And may Christ save thy soul!

"From Brigg o' Doom when thou art past,
    Every night and a',
To Purgatory thou 'll come at last,
    And may Christ save thy soul!

"If thou hast given victuals and drink,
    Every night and a',
The fire will not make thee shrink,
    And may Christ save thy soul!

"If victuals and drink thou hast given nane,
    Every night and a',
The fire will burn thee to the bare bane.
    And may Christ save thy soul!"

This innocent ballad — where it could have come from we cannot imagine — became especially terrifying after evil reports began to be common about the old woman. What was "Winney Muir"? Where was the "Brigg o' Doom"? There must have been some dark meaning to "fire and sleet and candle-light," — the words sounded ghostly.

Among the old woman's friends was the child of a very estimable family, a little girl who often carried her presents. On the day before Christmas this child went to the hut with presents, and told her of the common report that she was to be molested.

"What, child, have I ever done that they should harm me? I have had a hard life, child; and before God, child, I have nothing on my conscience. Why should they wish to harm me, and on such a night, — the one that I love most of all the year? It would make religion a mockery. It should be a time of peace."

A BAMBOO BRIDGE.

"They say that you can fly, Mother Hollander."

"Fly, child? I could no more fly than this hut that these hands have thatched for forty years. They are false, child,—all the stories that they tell of my poor, friendless life."

The old woman resolved to intercept Peter and his bride in the highway when they should go to be married, and to make an appeal for her old hut, which, with all its poverty, had become to her a part of her life.

It was a cold December day, with a high wind and a light snow. The coast was rimmed with ice, and the sea was white with breakers. The old woman waited for the bridal couple, standing by the roadside in the high wind and snow. She was so full of anxiety that she little heeded the weather.

Over her shoulders was a light shawl, and on her head was a large hood, the strings of which were pinned to her shawl for greater security against the gusts of wind. With her was her faithful cat, the terror of all superstitious villagers.

As the time approached for Peter to pass, her anxiety grew. She stood in the middle of the road, holding on to her thin shawl and great hood, which every gust of wind threatened to blow away.

The chaise at last swept along the curve of the coast, in view of the hut, but Peter did not notice the form in the dusk and storm.

"Molly," said he, "we are going to break up the witch's den after the party to-night. It is a shame that some man has not had the courage to do it before. I am going to do it in honor of our weddin'. This is the last night that this community shall be terrified and preyed upon by the Flying Dutchwoman."

"And you are to be the Saint George," said Molly, proudly.

But Peter did not understand classical allusions.

"The what?"

"The champion. But are you not afraid of the consequences?"

"What consequences? The man that is about to marry you, Molly, never yet feared the face of a mortality."

"But do you not fear spirits?"

"No. I once did, but I have thought it all out; a truly brave man fears nothing. I fear nothing, Molly, nothing. Why should I?"

"Then why do you trouble the old woman at all?"

Just here a dark object met his astonished eyes. What! He checked the horse and rode cautiously.

"What is that yonder?" he said to the bride.

"In front of Mary Hollander's?"

"Yes. Somethin' awful."

"It looks like the witch herself. Oh, Peter, I'm glad you are brave! You will need your courage now! Do you see how she moves, as though she had wings, — just as though she was goin' to fly? Do you really think that she *can* ?"

The horse saw the strange-looking object, and snorted, and then suddenly stopped. The fear of a man is strangely communicated to an animal, and the horse seemed to become possessed of his master's terror.

The old woman saw the horse stop, and with the wind blowing wildly through her hood and shawl, both of which flapped like wings, she slowly approached the stationary vehicle.

"Mercy! she's comin', sure as death!" said Peter.

"What is that following her? asked the bride, herself filled with alarm.

"Is it a dog?" asked Peter, evasively.

"No, a *cat*. *That* cat, too! She looks just as if she was going to fly. Oh, dear! this is awful, — on such a night, too. What shall we do?"

The old woman hobbled on, her hood and shawl still flying about like wings. Suddenly she stopped and lifted her arms. The horse rose on his hind legs and began to back.

"You must get out, Peter, and hold him by the bits."

"Get *out!*" — the words froze him to his very heart. Get out under such appalling circumstances as these! He would as soon have leaped straight over a precipice.

"*You* get out, Molly. It don't seem as though there was any need that *both* of us should be killed. She hasn't anything against you. I expect 'tis I she's after."

"Is that the kind of man you are, Peter Skillet? A great husband you would make! It is your business to get out and quiet the horse and protect me, whatever may come."

In the midst of this exciting dialogue there came a furious gust of wind across the sea. The old woman had lifted her hands to beckon the bridal couple to wait for an interview and to hear what she had to say. Thus unprotected, her hood and shawl, which were pinned together, were left to the mercy of the wind. They suddenly rose into the air.

"There, there! Oh, mercy! she's goin' to fly. What did I tell you? There, there! she's goin'. Oh that I should ever have lived to see this day! There she goes, sure enough, — her soul right out of her body! Let me get out of this, — I am going mad!"

The high wind had taken the poor old woman's hood and shawl into the

A ROADSIDE IN JAVA.

air, which Peter's imagination had transformed into her natural body or her spiritual body, — he did not stop to question which. He saw something going through the air, and he had not the slightest doubt that it was she. The wind spread out the black shawl and hood, and they seemed animated.

There was a loose cover on the back of the chaise. Peter put one foot through this, tearing it asunder like a wild man. In a moment, out of the back of the chaise he tumbled, exclaiming in great agitation, "Good-by, Molly; may the heavings protect you! She is n't after you, any way."

Sandhills rose from the beach, now covered with a light snow ice. Up these went Peter as though he was treading on air. He slipped once or twice, but recovered himself with an electrical motion. In a few minutes there was not so much as a speck of Peter on the earth, in the air, or in the sky.

The old woman came up to the chaise, seized the reins, and quieted the horse. Her head was bare, and her white hair blew about her head in the wind.

"Where has *he* gone?" she asked, — "he who was going to tear down my old hut to-night, on Christmas eve, and for why? Molly Smart, are you going to marry such a man as that? What have I ever done that a young man should wish to molest me, a poor lone woman?"

"They say that you are a witch, and can fly; and you terrify people, and harm the town."

"Molly Smart, it is cowards that fly. A true man has nothing to fear in this world or from any other. All the stories about my evil ways spring from the imaginations of evil hearts. It is only the wicked and cowardly who think that they see ghosts. No good man ever yet beheld an evil spirit. How the wind blows! and where are my bonnet and shawl?"

The old woman stood still holding the horse.

"I will turn him around, Molly, and you had better drive him home. Good-night, Molly. I hope that you may have better luck than to marry a man who would turn a poor old innocent woman out of her home on Christmas eve, for being a witch. If I were you, I would be ashamed to think that I ever started out into a wild storm on such an errand as that."

She turned the horse carefully round, and hobbled back to her hut.

Christmas day brought the wildest excitement to the little village. Peter had returned home and related his terrible adventures. He had seen the old woman "mount into the sky right before his own eyes," and had expected to have "been taken into the air bodily" after her. But he had escaped.

Molly, too, had returned home, and had told her own truly exasperating story. She never saw Peter again, but one day married an Episcopal minister who did not believe in witches.

Peter was prophetic. The village was never disturbed by any further reports of witchcraft after the events of that night were made clear; and the young men never molested the old woman. She became pitied, and humanely treated and cared for; and the awful stories of the Flying Dutchwoman became the humorous household tale of the quiet seafaring village.

The dreadful ballad, too, ceased to haunt the port. Kind hands brought their Christmas gifts to the hut, when the snows drifted over the kelp where had blossomed the morning-glories. She used to relate to them queer tales of the Ships of the Netherland Trading Company, and of the coffee, mountains, and ports of Java, — stories that she had heard her husband tell in the long-past years.

She was found, one winter day, dead on her bed in the cottage, with the faithful old cat asleep on her breast. Her lonely grave used to be seen in one corner of a windy burying-ground on the high coast near the fishing-town on Cape Ann.

The old martin-boxes are gone, and the swallows that recalled the bright voyages to Java no longer come on bright wings to the place. But the place still recalls to many minds the beautiful island of the far Indian sea, with its ships, its spices, and its coffee.

"PEOPLE SEEMED TO LIVE ON THE WATER."

CHAPTER XI.

BANGKOK.

I WILL pass over our voyage. We found ourselves, after some two months from Florida, safely housed in Bangkok, — Ivory in his own home, and I with him in the mission house.

Ivory's father made many private inquiries about him when we were alone. I had nothing but good to say of him, except that I would sometimes say, "I only wish that he was a more manly boy." Yet he was manly. It required really more courage to take a position which the popular mind held to be cowardly, than my opposite view.

Ivory entered into telegraph service in connection with a new line of railway in Siam. I was sent to Sumatra, as a lineman.

Bangkok, which Ivory has already described in his letters, was a surprise to me. Its life was unlike any other I had seen. People seemed to live on the water and in the air, — in floating houses and houses on poles.

I visited the temples of the Emerald and Sleeping Idols. The Emerald Idol is made of gold into which jewels — crystals, diamonds, sapphires, and rubies — were poured when the ore was in a melted state. The altar is a pyramid about a hundred feet high, blazing with gems and gold. The Sleeping Idol is one hundred and fifty feet long and forty high, and is wholly overlaid with gold. I had never dreamed of such splendors of superstition.

MRS. LEONOWENS IN THE "INNER CITY."

On the eastern side of the beautiful river Meinam is a vast plot of ground encompassed by two walls. These walls run parallel to each other, and are flanked on all sides with towers and fortresses. They are a little over a mile in length, and about three miles in circumference.

Inside of these walls stands the inner city, where reside none but women and children.

But this peculiar community is in many respects as self-supporting and as independent as any other in the world. It has its own peculiar laws, its women judges, Amazon guards, prisons, and executioners, who are women, traders, merchants, spinners, weavers; and almost every function is exercised by women, and by them only.

Into this city no man is permitted to enter except the ninety-nine priests of Buddha, who are admitted every morning, under guard, that the inmates may perform the sacred duty of giving alms.

On the eastern front of this walled enclosure rise, high above the trees, the many-towered and gilded roofs of the grand royal palace. Next to this is the old palace; and to both of these palaces is a private covered entrance for the women who attend upon the person of the King.

A few steps from this entrance blooms a beautiful flower-garden, filled with gorgeous tropical flowers. In the centre of this garden is a small, artificial lake. In this, as if to crown the beauty of the spot, the magnificent Victoria Regia, the queen of water-lilies, rises to the surface, spreads out her basin-like leaves, and opens her pure heart, surrounded by a hundred fragrant petals, to the sunrise, blushing a delicate pink at every petal-tip as she turns her wondrous face to the midday sun, and at evening closing as if for sorrow for her departed god.

Morning and evening the great ladies and princesses assemble to bathe in the lake, spending many an idle hour in its waters, rifling the water-lilies with which they delight in adorning themselves.

Hard by is a great pillared hall, in which the petty cases of theft, gambling, and other misdeeds committed by the women, are tried. Twelve women hold the position of judges in this inner city.

The floor of this judgment hall consists of trap-doors, which open to subterranean cells that are used as prisons for the women.

If a woman is found to have committed the slightest misdemeanor, the

"WITHIN THESE WALLS RESIDE NONE BUT WOMEN."

matter is instantly laid before the chief woman judge, Khoon Thou App, who gives the order of arrest to the Amazons, after which she is regularly sued for the offence, and is sometimes imprisoned in one of these underground dungeons.

No pen, no words, however graphic, can convey to your mind any idea of these terrible prisons. The feet sink into the floor, through the planks of which the river oozes upward. The atmosphere is pestilential. The walls are painted with humble representations of all kinds of suffering under tortures.

I remember I once missed a very interesting young woman, named Mai Prang, who was in the habit of visiting my school-room, and her dear little children missed her too. Day after day they vainly asked their old aunt,—

"When will mother come back?"

I was so touched and saddened by the sight of these apparently deserted children, that I inquired from one of my royal pupils what had become of Mai Prang.

To my surprise and horror, she made me a most significant sign. Placing her forefinger on her lips, she then drew it slowly across her throat, thereby intimating that the unhappy woman, for some unknown crime, had been secretly made away with.

Near the judgment hall is the beautiful temple of the "Mothers of the Free,"—that is, free from the superstitions of the Brahmins,—with antique style of architecture, and its long, dim gallery, in which I used to teach the royal children.

Next to this building is the theatre and the gymnasium, where the great ladies and princesses of the court assemble every afternoon to gossip, play games, and to watch the exercises of the dancing-girls.

Here are girls of all ages, from five to twenty, being drilled in dancing, to which particular attention is given, and also in a variety of other accomplishments. This is one of the most interesting sights in the inner city. All day long the girls are seen exercising. Some are poised on tip-toe, others bending their arms and limbs back as far as they will reach, and again others picking up bits of straw with their eyelids. This very curious and subtle feat can be learned only by very young girls, who are made to practise it in order to render them flexible in every part of the body.

There are two long rows of benches, one a little higher than the other. On the lower are placed a row of little girls, very scantily dressed, and on the upper bench are laid fine polished bits of straw. At the sound of the drum the little girls all together bend back the head and neck until they touch the bits of straw, and which with wonderful dexterity they secure between the corners of the eyelids. It often takes a young girl three or four years of constant practice to acquire this peculiar flexibility of form and movement.

Among others, the cup dance is the most graceful and poetic of their dances. A row of young women, with a tier of cups on their heads, take their places in the centre of the gymnasium. A burst of joyous music follows. On hearing this they simultaneously, with military precision, kneel down, fold their hands, bow till their foreheads almost touch the polished marble floor, keeping the cups steadily on their heads by some marvellous jerk of the neck. Then suddenly springing to their feet, they describe a succession of rapid and intricate circles, keeping time to the music with their arms, head, and feet.

Next follows a miracle of art such as may be found only among people of the highest physical training. The music swells into a rapturous tumult. The dancers raise their delicate feet, curve their arms and fingers in seemingly impossible flexures, sway to and fro like withes of willow, agitate all the muscles of the body like the flutter of leaves in a soft evening breeze, but still keep the tier of cups on their heads. These to the looker-on present the strange appearance of gliding about the dancers' arms and limbs as they float about the room.

At other times, a cup full of some liquid is placed on the floor in the centre of the hall. A girl will spring to her feet and dance about it in round wild eddies, and suddenly laying herself down, keeping her arms folded tight on her breast, will take up the cup with her lips, and drain the liquid without spilling a drop.

The temple of the "Mothers of the Free" occupies not only a central position, but is one of the most important buildings in this woman's city.

On the right of this building is a Japanese temple, perfect in style, and very exquisitely decorated within and without. Behind this is a very fine marble temple, newly erected, and designed for a great molten image of silver of the "Adhi Buddh," or Supreme Intelligence. There are a great many exquisite little pagodas round it, which add very much to the interest and beauty of this particular spot.

It was a very interesting sight to watch the inmates of this city assembling at morning prayers in this temple.

About nine o'clock every morning the innumerable little bells that surround the temples and pagodas were heard tinkling from far and near. The narrow, crooked streets and lanes which intersect and cross each other in the most bewildering irregularity are suddenly thronged with women and children of all ages, from the tottering, feeble old dame of eighty, to the two-year-old who is just beginning to feel the solid earth under her little feet.

SIAMESE DRAMATIC ARTISTS.

The princesses and ladies of high rank, dressed in many-colored silks, gay scarfs fluttering in the breeze, and laden with golden ornaments, each one followed by a host of female slaves, — some half nude, and others very neatly dressed, according to their circumstances, — bearing vases of flowers, perfumed tapers in golden candlesticks, and gold and silver tea-trays, with teapots and teacups all ready for use, form a brilliant part of the diversified procession.

In addition to these, every prince, princess, and great lady has an especial slave, whose duty it is to carry his or her betel box; for even while at prayers the Siamese may be seen chewing their betel, or indulging occasionally in a cup of tea.

The betel-tree is the areca palm of Linnæus. Its form is very slender; its trunk is remarkably upright and straight, without a knot or limb, until within one or two feet of its summit, when it branches out into a shower of from ten to fifteen long, graceful leaves drooping downward and upward. The fruit grows in large clusters, from one hundred and fifty to three hundred nuts depending from each cluster, each about the size and shape of a large plum. They prefer this nut in a fresh state. It is eaten with the cere-leaf, a perennial belonging to the pepper family, and red lime, — a curious preparation. Before the burnt limestone has been slackened, an infusion of tumeric is poured upon it, which causes it to fall into powder, taking a fine vermilion color. This plastic red lime is spread on the cere-leaf, and chewed much in the way of tobacco. In fact, the chewing of the betel compound has obtained the same power over the Siamese that tobacco has over the European race.

But to return to my subject.

As soon as the crowd arrive at the temple, the princes and princesses rank first in order. They take their seats near the pulpit, on the silken cushions placed for them on the tessellated floor of the temple.

After these come the great ladies and female officers of the inner court, then the wives of the King, and last of all the slaves. Before each and every worshipper stand golden vases filled with fresh, fragrant flowers, odoriferous tapers, and a small gift for the priests.

At the appointed hour the tinkling of the pagoda bells gently ceases. Two priests, attended by armed Amazons and fierce-looking eunuchs equipped with swords and staves, enter the temple at the eastern gate, veiling their faces with their jewelled fans, lest their eyes should wander towards any of the pretty women, and tempt their thoughts to stray from their sacred offices of prayer and praise.

The head priest mounts a heavily gilt pulpit, and the other takes his place on a raised platform behind it.

The Siamese pulpit, by the way, is very unlike those used in our places of worship. It is more like a throne of state. It has a high, circular back, richly carved and gilt, and towering at least four feet above the head of the priest, and enclosing him on the right and left. On the steps are engraved passages from the Buddhist Scriptures; and the whole is supported on the tails of four open-mouthed dragons, which form the pedestals, producing a weird and grotesque effect.

The sacred books of the Buddhists are composed of long strips of ancient palm-leaves. The characters are in Pali, — which is the language of the Buddhists' books of Ceylon, corrupted by oral and perhaps provincial use from the more perfect and polished Sanskrit, — pricked in by means of a stylus, and then traced over with dyes of various hues, red, blue, and yellow. The edges are often beautifully illuminated with curious designs.

The moment the priest has unrolled the pale yellow leaves of his palm manuscript, the assembled company of high and lowly born women and children raise themselves on their knees, light their tapers, place them on either side of their flowers, fold their hands, and assume with closed eyes the most reverent attitude of worship. Many of them kneel throughout the service.

There is, first, a liturgy in which the congregation joins, and then a sermon from some Buddhist text. After the service the princesses and the great ladies crawl on all fours towards the pulpit, and present their little gifts to the priests. These are taken in charge by the eunuch and handed to the priests' attendants, who are in waiting without the gates of the inner city.

Another curious custom is that of sprinkling this woman's city with holy water, in order to drive away the evil spirits who are supposed to infest the atmosphere. About two o'clock in the afternoon a company of priests, closely guarded, enter the city at one gate. They are furnished with pots of consecrated water and branches of acacia. They dip these into the water, and scatter purifying showers here, there, and everywhere, and pass out by another gate. This custom was a source of great annoyance to me, as no sooner did the priests appear than my pupils made a frantic rush, often in the midst of their recitations, to prostrate themselves on the pavement within reach of these purifying showers.

The ladies of the harem have each an annual salary and a private residence assigned to them within these walls, where they live exactly in the condition of State prisoners. They are each one and all obliged to appear handsomely dressed, once a day at least, at the King's palace, to wait upon his pleasure, where he converses with them or not according to his moods. On these occasions several hundred women and children are found seated in the alcoves and

THE CEREMONIAL OF SHAVING THE HAIR.

shadowy recesses of the "Kinkaub" curtains. Women officers are in waiting. If there should happen to be too much giggling and whispering from behind these curtains, a female officer will start up and lay the whip lightly on the shoulders of some of the most noisy. I have known the whip to be administered three times during one of these audiences. The moment the King turns his back, they scatter like a flock of wild geese, and rush away to their respective homes, having got through an unpleasant duty.

The King seldom visits the ladies of the harem. On the occasion of the birth of a child, or when the infant is about to be named, he does so, however, with great pomp and ceremony. The streets, which in some parts are wretchedly dirty, are swept clean. The women and slaves all turn out and prostrate themselves along the sidewalks. The poor mother greets him kneeling on the threshold of her home with the royal babe in her arms. He takes the child, embraces it, and returns it to her accompanied with costly gifts and presents, if she happens to be a favorite; if not, some little trinket or toy.

A female barber and some priests, strictly guarded, are finally ushered into an open hall which adjoins each house. The babe is handed to the lady barber, who shaves the hair, leaving only a small tuft on the top of the child's head. She then transfers the infant to the priest, who pours on its bald head a pot of consecrated water, while the King repeats aloud the name the child is to bear through life.

All the markets and shops, and even some of the mechanical trades, are in the hands of the slave-women, who spend much of their time within the walls of this city, but who have homes and husbands outside of the walls.

The devotion of some of the Buddhist women as wives and mothers is very remarkable. Sir John Bowring, and many other distinguished travellers, have observed that they are infinitely more moral and industrious than the rest of their Asiatic sisters. Mrs. Smith, a missionary lady, once accompanied me to the stall of a pretty little flower-woman; and when she spoke to her of heaven and hell, the poor woman said she could not make up her mind to which of the worlds she would go, but would go out of the city and talk to her husband. "If he will go to your heaven," said she, "I will go with him; but if he *will* go to that other world, I shall wish to go and live with him there, to wash and take care of him."

Before carrying my narrative to Sumatra, I must relate the story of a figure whose hideousness excited my curiosity whenever I met it;

and I found it often in a week's rambles among the temples and sacred places of Bangkok.

THE STORY OF THE HOALAMAN.

The Hoalaman was an odd divinity, half man and half beast, of great power and wisdom.

When a certain phya, or lord, was about to found a new city, afterward Ayathia, in the dim times when strange divinities mingled with men, he was directed to shoot an arrow into the air, and to break the ground where it should fall.

He did so. A hoalaman caught the arrow, carried to the fortunate place, and stuck it into the ground.

Then the creature's tail began to grow, and it formed a coil of immense length.

The phya came to the hoalaman.

"The city may be as large as the circumference that can be marked by my tail," said the creature.

The tail grew and grew. What became of it, the legend does not tell.

But the hoalaman promised that if the city was ever in peril and needed assistance, he would come again.

"This shall be the sign," said the god: "you shall beat a drum."

The people remembered the promise and felt secure. But in the process of time they began to doubt the hoalaman.

"Let us beat the drum," said the sceptics, "and see if he will appear."

So it was agreed that there should be a festival to try the hoalaman, and that the drum should be beaten.

It was a bright day, and a splendid assembly. The drum was beaten, and soon a gigantic figure darkened the air.

"What will you have?" asked the hoalaman.

"Nothing," said the priests. "We only wished to test you to see if you would come."

The hoalaman's face grew dark and angry. He rose o'er the city, and flew away in the gathering clouds.

War came, and famine, and there was great distress. The people called on the priests to beat the drum for the hoalaman.

The priests did so. The people waited, but nothing appeared. The drum

HE SHOT AN ARROW INTO THE AIR.

has been beaten many times since in peril, but he has never appeared again. And it was very long ago when he is said to have appeared.

Still among the festivals of Bangkok, the new royal city, is one to the hoalaman. Whether he will ever appear again, we cannot say. But we give his picture, which will show you how he did appear. Whose thought created him, we cannot tell. No one knows; but all architectural embellishments of stone and marble were once some one's thoughts, and most thoughts in marble are the poetry of the past.

CHAPTER XII.

THE SIAMESE TWINS.

NEARLY everybody is interested in the wonders of Nature, whether they are simply animals that are rarely seen, or what are called freaks of Nature; that is, unusually large, or uncommonly small, or curiously developed specimens of common animals. We all like to see giants, and dwarfs, and the strange creatures of the menagerie.

The Siamese twins, Chang and Eng, who died on the 17th of January, 1874, belonged to the class of strangely developed human beings, and they were interesting mainly, but not wholly, on that account. They were two men joined together from their birth and all through life. The breast-bone of each was prolonged in the form of a hard, stiff substance, called cartilage, which connected them together, making them curiously one, while they were also two persons.

Chang and Eng were found, about the year 1829, in a village of Siam, by a sea-captain from Newburyport, Mass. They were then supposed to be about eighteen years old. Their mother had seventeen children, but they alone were in any way different from ordinary Siamese children.

Captain Coffin, the sea-captain who found the two boys in Siam, bought them from their parents, who were very poor people, and, taking them on board his ship, brought them to this country. Here

they excited a good deal of interest. They were carried about from place to place, and exhibited to large numbers of people.

Afterwards they gave exhibitions on their own account, and made a handsome property. With this they bought a farm in North Carolina, on which they lived. Two women, sisters, consented to marry them, and the two families lived together under the same roof. During the Civil War they remained at home undisturbed; but the war made them poor, and they were compelled in 1866 to travel and exhibit themselves once more. Then they again returned to North Carolina, and remained there until their death.

THE SIAMESE TWINS.
(From Johnson's Encyclopædia.)

That which seemed to excite the most wonder in the minds of those who saw them, but which was really one of the least wonderful things about them, was that they appeared always to think alike and to act alike. When they were coming over from Siam the sailors used to play with them and chase them around the ship. One day, in running to escape from their pursuers, they came to an open hatchway; if they had tumbled into the hold of the vessel, they would have been killed. They both leaped at the same instant, and landed safely on the other side.

Among other things, scientific men tried to decide whether their likeness in thought and action was caused by their being joined together; that is, whether it was because they had, as it were, only one body. The general opinion was that such was not the cause, but that their harmony was the result of habit. From infancy they had been obliged to do the same thing. Nothing could have been more foolish than a quarrel between them, and they had simply learned, by doing the same thing at the same time, to think and act alike, as two most intimate friends. Yet there was a real connection between them that partly explains this harmony, notwithstanding the opinion of scientific men. Their hearts beat at the same rate and at the same instant, and they breathed also exactly alike. There was a point in the centre of the link that bound them together, and for an inch on either side, where, if a pin were stuck into the skin, both would feel it; this proves that the nerves of the two men were connected, and the nerves are only an extension of the brain. Consequently the brains of the two — the brain being the origin of thought and act — were joined.

It was always a very interesting question whether either of the twins could continue to live if the connection should be cut. When Chang and Eng were in Europe some years ago, very eminent surgeons were consulted on this point. The twins submitted to some experiments intended to settle the question. One of these was tying a cord very tightly around the substance that joined them. They both showed signs of distress, and came very near fainting. From this it was concluded that they could not be cut apart and live, although a few physicians declared that it would be possible; but all advised that if either should die, the bond between the living and dead should be severed at once.

The twins themselves, however, secretly determined not to act on this advice. They directed by their wills that they should never be parted, even in death. It would probably have been impossible for either to live without the companionship of the other, even if there had been a possibility of mere existence when they had been separated. But evidently they had agreed that neither wished to survive the other.

It was surprising what these two men could do in spite of their

JAVAN WOMEN DANCING.

being held so closely together. They could turn back to back, or face to face, with but little inconvenience; one could stand on a stool while the other was on the floor. They were able to do the ordinary work on a farm; and although together they could perform more than the labor of one man, they could not perform the labor of two.

They were possessed of a very good degree of intelligence. Even on the passage to this country, they learned to play checkers well enough to defeat some old players. They learned our language, and became good American citizens. Some years ago they united with a Baptist church in North Carolina; and although they were not without some serious faults, they were regarded as, on the whole, consistent church-members.

Other persons joined together as curiously as they, have been known to exist, but never before did any twins so connected live to such an age. They were supposed to have been born in 1811, and they were therefore about sixty-three years old when they died; and it does not seem that their peculiar condition had anything to do with causing the death of Chang.

The later history of these two remarkable brothers was very sad. Their wives, though sisters, did not agree, and finally one of them left the house where they had all lived together. There were six children in one family and five in the other. A part of these were both deaf and dumb, and the rest were not bright.

These domestic troubles caused the brothers to become somewhat estranged. It would be hard to conceive of any situation more distressing than to be compelled always to be in the company of a person with whom one is not on the best of terms. Finally, Chang was attacked by paralysis, and, like many another, he took to intoxicating drink to allay his suffering. He grew worse, and at last, on the morning of the 17th of January, 1874, he died.

When Eng discovered that his life-long companion was dead, he was filled with such agony and dread that he became deranged. His violent insanity soon changed to insensibility, and in about two hours after Chang's death he breathed his last. The grief of the two wives and of the partially idiotic children is said to have been very touching.

The most remarkable thing about the Siamese twins, after all, is that they were able to overcome to so great an extent the restraints which Nature had put upon them. That which made them differ from other men hindered them also in doing what other men do. They succeeded in conquering Nature as really as the blind man does when he learns to see with his fingers, or as the dumb child does when he learns to hear with his eyes. They might have been contented to live at ease by showing their peculiarity. They chose, instead, to earn a living as other men do. For this they were entitled to credit, and to be remembered with respect, as men who, under difficult circumstances, tried to act well their part.

A JAVAN HOME.

CHAPTER XIII.

THE ADVENTURES OF A LINEMAN IN SUMATRA.

HE Indian is, perhaps, the only ocean known to ancient history. It is certain that the navies of King Solomon entered it and found some of the riches of its coast.

It is an ocean of islands, — of a thousand islands which are little continents; of ten thousand islands, if we count the gardens of the warm sea. It washes the palm-shaded shores of Africa, Arabia, Persia, and India, and the East India islands, Australia, and Van Diemen's Land. Many of its groups of islands are like cities of the sea, — Venices and Bangkoks. Among its islands are wild Madagascar and beautiful Ceylon.

The stories of the sea which for centuries have delighted the world and excited its wonder, have been largely associated with these islands. Christianity has been carried to them all. There has followed the missionary two potent forces and coadjutors of civilization, — steam and electricity. The section hands and the linemen have been the missionaries of civilization. Next to heart and thought and the Divine inspiration, these two forces — steam and electricity, the engine and the telegraph — have most greatly changed the islands of the sea. The steam-engine may be said to govern them all.

The work of the lineman has received but little credit in the history of recent progress; but barbarism has disappeared wherever this persevering individual has stretched the line that makes the lightning the servant of human thought.

The increase of telegraph communication is the wonder of the age. New York can talk with India in a few hours. In 1880, 31,700,000 telegrams were sent in the United States. Fifteen thousand people were employed in telegraphy by the same census. Of these about 2,500 were linesmen, or linemen.

A lineman is one who runs telegraph wires. The business requires special scientific training. In many distant places the telegraph line has to be protected and often mended. In Asia the lineman, like the section hand on the railway, finds constant service. Asia is being covered with railroads and telegraph lines, and especially India, and the provinces under the English and French flags. Submarine cables connect the islands of the East Indies, and the islands themselves are crossed by commercial wires.

The linemen, like the section hands, in Asiatic countries are mostly English. It requires an army of English laborers to build and protect the ways and communications of commerce.

Among the many destructive agents of the telegraph in Asiatic countries and islands are elephants and apes.

Dr. C. A. Stephens, in the "Youth's Companion," has given a series of articles on the perils of a lineman's life, in which the lineman has the following experience with elephants: —

ROGUISH ELEPHANTS.

During the year I was in this Sumatran company's employ, my duties led me to reside at a station called Gunong Lobo, where the line crosses one of the military roads which the Dutch have built and maintain across the island. At this station were four *rumahs* (pole-houses), elevated on posts, the better to keep out vermin and wild beasts, and occupied by a lieutenant and a squad of native soldiers, who each serve three months of the year.

Near these was placed the new telegraph office where I had my quarters; and with me my one assistant, a Sumatran Malay boy, named Udong, who was certainly one of the most peculiar youngsters ever described.

"DOWN THE VALLEY OF THE RIVER BUSAR."

Udong hailed from one of the southern *kampongs*, up the river Inem from Palembang. He was not far from seventeen years of age, and looked very much like a Chinaman, his complexion being only a trifle darker and more sallow, and his eyes rather less oblique.

He always wore a gay but dirty print tunic, wide blue trousers, and a big sun-hat of palm-leaf which he made himself. Of all the boys I ever met, he was the softest-spoken, as well as the mildest and slowest. He was slow to move, slow to speak, and slow to understand,— particularly slow to understand anything he did not wish to do.

At such times he would stand stock-still and look the picture of amiability, not to say silliness, while you told him ten or twelve times what you wished him to do; then he would sit down and sigh. If, out of all patience, you spoke sharply, he would look up and smile with winning sweetness.

It was of no use trying to avoid it; I was obliged to punish him about once a week. It seemed as if it required a moderately severe beating to key him up. He would stand in passive expectation of it, never run away, nor try to escape till I let go of his collar.

Then he would run with all his might, with a horrified face turned back over his left shoulder,— always the left,— and his coarse black hair rising straight up from his head.

In three minutes he would come back, however, and do his work with perfect decorum. He really was quite *fond of me!*

The reader may think that Udong was a fool; but he was far from that. He was merely a *Malay;* and he knew a great deal, in a Malay way, and would say and do uncommonly bright things. His nose was crooked to one side, and one of his legs presented a curious spectacle from the deep-pitted scars where a tiger had "chewed" it some ten years previously.

There were rather over twenty miles of wire in the section which I had to keep in order, stretching southward from Gunong Lobo down the valley of the river Busar,— a beautiful region of country, walled on the east by several high peaks, from one of which rose constantly, in fair weather, a tall white column of smoke.

But if storms were at hand, the smoke would grow black and hang in an immense sable cloud, like an inverted cone, over the mountain. The natives call this volcano Benu Sorboro. It came to be my weather prophet, taking the place of "Probabilities."

The second week after I went upon duty there, a cyclone passed over the island, tearing a "road" through the forests, and prostrating fully a mile of posts and wire. In the case of such "breaks," I generally took Udong along with me, to carry wire and a little bag of "insulators," and also to assist in cutting away overblown trees and putting up fallen poles.

A telegraph line through such a country needs a great deal of looking after. Trees — all vegetation, in fact — grow very rapidly and rankly in these sub-tropic islands, and tornadoes are of almost weekly occurrence.

A LITTLE SUSPENSION BRIDGE OF BAMBOO.

Along the Busar there was a rich growth of cocoanut, areca, palmetto, and other palms, rising erect and tall from amidst a dense undergrowth of creeping, prickly-leaved rattan, trailing calamus, and stiff, rigid bamboo.

A roadway fifty feet wide had been "bushed" out for the telegraph wires, but the lofty cocoanut-trees often fell across this space. The sun bears kill a great many of these noble palms, climbing up and eating the "cabbage" bud at the top, after which the trunk falls in a few years.

But falling trees were far from being our worst and most dangerous adversaries. Toward the latter part of my first month there, a herd of elephants came over into the valley from the interior districts of the island, where these great animals are said to be numerous.

It is what naturalists rank as the *Elephas Sumatrensis*, and is held to differ

A SCENE IN SUMATRA.

somewhat from both the African and Asiatic species. Be that as it may, these Sumatran elephants are the most cunning, bothersome brutes it has ever been my lot to meet.

The first intimation I had of their presence on the Busar was a "break" of the line. Very early one morning the operator up at Padang began calling Gunong Lobo, and upon my responding, declared there was a "break" between me and Ari Pusu, the station next below.

This I at once found to be true. Ari Pusu was "dead." No business could be done between Padang and Batavia till the break was mended. So I at once roused out Udong, and we set off down the line afoot; for the company did not provide horses.

It was hardly light, but the *munyeets* (monkeys) were chattering and the parrots had begun to scream. We went rapidly down the line, along the cleared "lane," keeping directly under the wires, so as to see, by looking up at them against the sky, that they were in place on the glasses. We had proceeded three or four miles, when Udong suddenly stopped and pulled my blouse-sleeve.

"Heer! Heer!" he whispered, in his softest of whispers, — he always addressed me as *Heer*, which was his Malayan pronunciation of the Dutch *Herr*, or "sir."

"Heer, moluk cer kripuse esp zoochese gigi!" which I may freely translate into, "Sir, sir, I smell the huge beasts!" By "huge beasts" he meant elephants, as I well knew.

Udong had a keener sense of smell than I; for though I sniffed this way and that, I could smell nothing, save the great rank narka blossoms.

But as I had some confidence in the lad's nasal powers, we proceeded rather more cautiously, Udong telling me that probably there had been *sarkawok*-war — that is to say, elephant-war — over in the interior, among the great herds there, and that some had been driven forth as exiles.

These banished ones had, in the lad's opinion, come through the mountain-passes to the Busar. Terrible *sarkawoks*, he assured me, sometimes raged between different tribes of elephants, particularly after some old *bagut* (king-elephant) had died, or been killed.

As soon as day had fairly dawned, the tracks of elephants — not less than fifteen of them — were plainly visible in the open lane along the wires, as also heaps of their coarse excrement. But these tracks were all on the east side of the line.

The animals appeared to have followed one after the other, in single file, keeping to the lane, but going on as much aloof from the pendent wires as possible. There was not a track either beneath the wires or on the other side of them.

Udong at once bade me notice this circumstance, saying, "*Geezu* him 'fraid trap;" meaning that the elephants suspected that the wires were some snare laid for them.

Yet they enjoyed the easy, open route along the cleared "lane" too well to leave it; or perhaps, as I now surmise, they wished to go farther to the west, and having come to the wires and not daring to pass beneath them, they were following along the line, expecting presently to come to the end of it, and so go around it.

It shows how keen are the senses of these creatures, and how distrustful and sagacious are their minds, that they should, on approaching the line at dead of night, at once have discovered it and formed such an opinion of it.

Following on the trail of the herd, we came, just at sunrise, to a large creek, which flows down from the hills into the Busar. A little suspension-bridge of rattans had been hung over the creek at this point.

The elephants had torn this bridge down and forded the stream; and Udong tells me that whenever a herd follows along any of the island roads or paths, they invariably destroy the bridges before crossing the creeks or rivers, and that they cause the native planters and others a vast deal of trouble in this respect.

After crossing the creek we climbed a long stretch of upland for half an hour or more, but immediately, on gaining the height of land overlooking a considerable valley beyond, Udong, who was a few rods ahead, turned back, exclaiming, —

"Ahk geezu ekki, Heer! Ahk mu gie kissu O, Heer!" (Here are the elephants, sir! Here are the big rogues!)

Hurrying forward and glancing down the long lane, I saw a truly strange sight, — one that filled me at once with both astonishment and anxiety.

Half or three-fourths of a mile down the lane were the elephants, fifteen or sixteen of them, all busy as bees, tearing down the telegraph posts and wires!

Evidently they had grown tired of trying to go round the line, and had set to work to demolish it.

Already, as I could see, they had six or eight hundred yards of it down; and from the sturdy manner in which they were delving away, it looked as if, not content with merely making a gap, they had determined to tear down the entire line.

But could I for a moment have divested my mind of my great anxiety and sense of responsibility, it would have been a most interesting spectacle. It was

"OTHERS WERE BREAKING DOWN OR WRENCHING OUT THE POSTS."

a Titanic job, and these huge animal Titans were at it after a Samsonian fashion all their own.

Three or four were reaching up and tugging back at the wires with their trunks, — wrenching down length after length. Others seemed to be coiling, or wadding up, long stretches of wire already hauled down and broken off.

These bent and crinkled-up masses they marched off with, holding them aloft; and I could see that some went to the river, while others went back into the forest.

Still others were breaking down or wrenching out the posts, kneeling and twisting at them with their trunks or tusks. I could distinctly hear the poles crack.

Indeed, there was a considerable hubbub; and over the noise of their labor would resound, here and there, a loud trumpet-like squeak, as of savage glee and exultation over the havoc they were making.

I scarcely knew what to do. Glancing at Udong, I noticed in his commonly mild, immobile face a gleam of unwonted fun and excitement.

"Is your gun loaded, Udong?" I exclaimed.

"Jak! jak!" said he, eagerly.

"Will you make fight, Udong? Will you come snug after me and not run off?" I questioned.

"Jak! jak! No run!"

I argued from this readiness that Udong did not deem the herd very dangerous, and started down the hill, putting fresh cartridges into my carbine as we went along.

Coming within three hundred yards of the nearest of the troop, I first looked out a good place to send into the thick rattans, then bade Udong fire his old Dutch musket at the elephants and yell as loud as he could.

I followed suit with my Spencer carbine, peppering the nearest of the big brutes where they stood tugging at a post.

With the first bang of Udong's old gun and the sharp reports of my breech-loader, the whole herd stopped work and faced about.

I expected nothing but that they would charge on us. They stared for an instant, their great ears rising; then such a trumpeting rose as might have been heard five miles.

We fired several more shots, when to my surprise and great relief, the entire troop made off, racing down across the intervale to the Busar, which they crossed at a place where the water was so deep that we could see nothing of them in the stream save the ends of their trunks, held up — Udong said — to breathe by. They kept up a savage trumpeting, but on emerging from the river, made off into the woods beyond it.

Not less than a thousand yards of the line was demolished, wires and posts. After a hurried survey of the "break," I sent Udong back to the station, bidding him get the lieutenant and his men, and return with all the spare wire and insulators. I then fell to work to do what I could, alone, till they came, hoping to get at least one wire working across the gap by nightfall.

Noon came. Udong did not come. I worked on alone till past five o'clock; then, quite tired out and faint with hunger, I made my way back to the station.

Udong was asleep. He had eaten up all the cooked food we had, and gone to bed; and he had not *said a word to the lieutenant*. But I was too much fatigued and too faint to disturb the serenity of his dreams that night.

It was thirty-six hours before we had the line working again; and this was far from being the last of our troubles with the elephants.

The Indian Sea islands are full of charming tales. The old Mohammedan legends are told there, — stories as bejewelled with radiant fancies as the Arabian Nights. Two kinds of tales enchant all people of these antipodal palm-lands, — those of the Caliphs of Persia and those of the Rajahs of India. Many of these stories are allegories of life. We give one which illustrates, in a very humorous way, the life of a class of people whom circumstances make to pass for more than they are worth. We have never found a more clever illustration of the ridiculous manner in which one may gain a false reputation.

A MAN WHO SCARED AN ARMY.

ABRIDGED FROM "OLD DECCAN DAYS."

Once upon a time, in a violent storm of thunder, lightning, wind, and rain, a Tiger crept for shelter close to the wall of an old woman's hut.

At this moment a Chattee-maker, or Potter, who was in search of his donkey which had strayed away, came down the road. The night being very cold, he had, truth to say, taken a little more toddy than was good for him, and seeing, by the light of a flash of lightning, a large animal lying down close to the old woman's hut, he mistook it for the donkey he was looking for. So running up to the Tiger, he seized hold of it by one ear, and commenced beating, kicking, and abusing it with all his might and main.

"You wretched creature!" he cried, "is this the way you serve me, obliging me to come out and look for you in such pouring rain and on such a dark night as this? Get up instantly, or I'll break every bone in your body!" So he went on scolding and thumping the Tiger with his utmost power, for he had worked himself up into a terrible rage. The Tiger did not know what to make of it all.

The Chattee-maker, having made the Tiger get up, got on his back and forced him to carry him home, kicking and beating him the whole way, for all this time he fancied he was on his donkey; and then he tied his fore feet and his head firmly together, and fastened him to a post in front of his house, and when he had done this he went to bed.

Next morning, when the Chattee-maker's wife got up and looked out of the window, what did she see but a great big Tiger tied up in front of their house,

"SO HE SENT FOR HIS LORDS AND ATTENDANTS, AND THEY ALL SET OFF TOGETHER."

to the post to which they usually fastened the donkey? She was very much surprised, and running to her husband awoke him, saying,—

"Do you know what animal you fetched home last night?"

"Yes; the donkey, to be sure," he answered.

"Come and see!" said she; and she showed him the great Tiger tied to the post. The Chattee-maker at this was no less astonished than his wife, and felt himself all over to find if the Tiger had not wounded him. But no! there he was safe and sound, and there was the Tiger tied to the post, just as he had fastened it up the night before.

News of the Chattee-maker's exploit soon spread through the village, and all the people came to see him and hear him tell how he had caught the Tiger and tied it to the post; and this they thought so wonderful that they sent a deputation to the Rajah, or King, with a letter to tell him how a man of their village had, alone and unarmed, caught a great Tiger and tied it to a post.

When the Rajah read the letter he also was much surprised, and determined to go in person and see this astonishing sight. So he sent for his lords and attendants, and they all set off together to look at the Chattee-maker and the Tiger he had caught.

Now, the Tiger was a very large one, and had long been the terror of all the country round, which made the whole matter still more extraordinary; and all this being represented to the Rajah, he determined to confer all possible honor on the valiant Chattee-maker. So he gave him houses and lands, and as much money as would fill a well, made him a lord of his court, and conferred on him the command of ten thousand horse.

It came to pass, shortly after this, that a neighboring Rajah, who had long had a quarrel with this one, sent to announce his attention of going instantly to war with him; and tidings were at the same time brought that the Rajah who sent the challenge had gathered a great army together on the borders, and was prepared at a moment's notice to invade the country.

In this dilemma no one knew what to do. The Rajah sent for all his generals, and inquired of them which would be willing to take command of his forces and oppose the enemy. They all replied that the country was so ill-prepared for the emergency, and the case was apparently so hopeless, that they would rather not take the responsibility of the chief command. The Rajah knew not whom to appoint in their stead. Then some of his people said to him, —

"You have lately given the command of ten thousand horse to the valiant Chattee-maker who caught the Tiger; why not make him commander-in-chief? A man who could catch a Tiger and tie him to a post, must surely be more courageous and clever than most."

"Very well," said the Rajah, "I will make him commander-in-chief." So he sent for the Chattee-maker and said to him, "In your hands I place all the power of the kingdom; you must put our enemies to flight for us."

"So be it," answered the Chattee-maker; "but before I lead the whole army against the enemy, suffer me to go by myself and examine their position, and, if possible, find out their numbers and strength."

The Rajah consented, and the Chattee-maker returned home to his wife, and said, —

"They have made me commander-in-chief, which is a very difficult post for me to fill, because I shall have to ride at the head of all the army, and you know I never was on a horse in my life. But I have succeeded in gaining a little delay, as the Rajah has given me permission to go first alone and reconnoitre the enemy's camp. Do you therefore provide a very quiet pony, for you know I cannot ride, and I will start to-morrow morning."

But before the Chattee-maker had started, the Rajah sent over to him a most magnificent charger richly caparisoned, which he begged he would ride when going to see the enemy's camp. The Chattee-maker was frightened almost out of his life, for the charger that the Rajah had sent him was very powerful and spirited, and he felt sure that even if he ever got on it, he should very soon tumble off; however, he did not dare to refuse it, for fear of offending the Rajah by not accepting his present. So he sent back to him a message of thanks, and said to his wife, —

"I cannot go on the pony, now that the Rajah has sent me this fine horse; but how am I ever to ride it?"

"Oh! don't be frightened," she answered; "you've only got to get upon it and I will tie you firmly on, so that you cannot tumble off; and if you start at night, no one will see that you are tied on."

"Very well," he said. So that night his wife brought the horse that the Rajah had sent him to the door.

"Indeed," said the Chattee-maker, "I can never get into that saddle, it is so high up."

"You must jump," said his wife.

So he tried to jump several times, but each time he jumped he tumbled down again.

"I always forget when I am jumping," said he, "which way I ought to turn."

"Your face must be toward the horse's head," she answered.

"To be sure, of course," he cried; and giving one great jump he jumped into the saddle, but with his face toward the horse's tail.

"This won't do at all," said his wife, as she helped him down again; "try getting on without jumping."

"I never can remember," he continued, "when I have got my left foot in the stirrup, what to do with my right foot or where to put it."

"That must go in the other stirrup," she answered; "let me help you."

So, after many trials, in which he tumbled down very often, for the horse was fresh and did not like standing still, the Chattee-maker got into the saddle; but no sooner had he got there than he cried, "Oh, wife, wife! tie me very firmly as quickly as possible, for I know I shall jump down if I can."

Then she fetched some strong rope and tied his feet firmly into the stirrups, and fastened one stirrup to the other, and put another rope round his waist and

"ON HE RODE AS FAST AS BEFORE, WITH THE TREE IN HIS HAND."

another round his neck, and fastened them to the horse's body and neck and tail.

When the horse felt all these ropes about him he could not imagine what queer creature had got upon his back, and he began rearing and kicking and prancing, and at last set off full gallop, as fast as he could tear, right across country.

"Wife, wife!" cried the Chattee-maker, "you forgot to tie my hands."

"Never mind," said she; "hold on by the mane."

So he caught hold of the horse's mane as firmly as he could.

Then away went horse, away went Chattee-maker, — away, away, away, over hedges, over ditches, over rivers, over plains, — away, away, like a flash of lightning, — now this way, now that, — on, on, on, gallop, gallop, gallop, — until they came in sight of the enemy's camp.

The Chattee-maker did not like his ride at all; and when he saw where it was leading him he liked it still less, for he thought the enemy would catch him and very likely kill him. So he determined to make one desperate effort to be free, and, stretching out his hand as the horse shot past a young banyan-tree, seized hold of it with all his might, hoping that the resistance it offered might cause the ropes that tied him to break. But the horse was going at his utmost speed, and the soil in which the banyan-tree grew was loose; so that when the Chattee-maker caught hold of it and gave it such a violent pull, it came up by the roots, and on he rode as fast as before, with the tree in his hand.

All the soldiers in the camp saw him coming, and, having heard that an army was to be sent against them, made sure that the Chattee-maker was one of the vanguard.

"See!" cried they: "here comes a man of gigantic stature on a mighty horse. He rides at full speed across the country, tearing up the very trees in his rage. He is one of the opposing force; the whole army must be close at hand. If they are such as he, we are all dead men."

Then, running to their Rajah, some of them cried again, "Here comes the whole force of the enemy," — for the story had by this time become exaggerated. "they are men of gigantic stature, mounted on mighty horses; as they come they tear up the very trees in their rage. We can oppose men, but not monsters such as these."

These were followed by others, who said, "It is all true," — for by this time the Chattee-maker had got pretty near the camp. "They're coming! they're coming! Let us fly! let us fly! Fly, fly for your lives!" And the whole panic-stricken multitude fled from the camp (those who had seen no cause for alarm going because the others did, or because they did not care to stay by themselves), after having obliged their Rajah to write a letter to the one whose country he was about to invade, to say that he would not do so, and propose terms of peace, and to sign it and seal it with his seal. Scarcely had all the people fled from the camp, when the horse on which the Chattee-maker was, came galloping into it; and on his back rode the Chattee-maker, almost dead from fatigue, with the banyan-tree in his hand. Just as he reached the camp, the ropes by which he was tied broke, and he fell to the ground. The horse stood still, too tired with his long run to go farther. On recovering his senses, the Chattee-maker found, to his surprise, that the whole camp, full of rich arms, clothes, and trappings, was entirely deserted. In the principal tent, moreover, he found a letter addressed to his Rajah, announcing the retreat of the invading army and proposing terms of peace.

So he took the letter, and returned home with it as fast as he could, leading his horse all the way, for he was afraid to mount him again. It did not take him long to reach his house by the direct road, for whilst riding he had gone a more circuitous journey than was necessary, and he got there just at nightfall. His wife ran out to meet him, overjoyed at his speedy return. As soon as he saw her, he said, —

"Ah, wife, since I saw you last I've been all round the world, and had many wonderful and terrible adventures. But never mind that now; send this letter quickly to the Rajah by a messenger, and send the horse also that he sent for me to ride. He will then see, by the horse looking so tired, what a long ride I've had; and if he is sent on beforehand, I shall not be obliged to ride him up to the palace door to-morrow morning, as I otherwise should, and that would be very tiresome, for most likely I should tumble off." So his wife sent the horse and the letter to the Rajah, and a message that her husband would be at the palace early next morning, as it was then late at night. And next day he went down there, as he had said he would; and when the people saw him coming, they said, "This man is as modest as he is brave; after having put our enemies to flight, he walks quite simply to the door, instead of riding here in state, as another man would," — for they did not know that the Chattee-maker walked because he was afraid to ride.

The Rajah came to the palace door to meet him, and paid him all possible honor. Terms of peace were agreed upon between the two countries, and the Chattee-maker was rewarded for all he had done by being given twice as much rank and wealth as he had before; and he lived very happily all the rest of his life.

AN AVENUE IN BATAVIA.

CHAPTER XIV.

JAVA, AND THE FLYING DUTCHMAN.

HE Javan boatmen played merrily in the shallow harbor, as the boats from our ship approached Batavia.

The music was peculiar. The song was called "Push and Row," and the thought is expressed in the music.

In the distance the tune became weird and beautiful. The ear followed it as if it were enchantment; and following the music we slowly drew near the river.

Then the music changed. The new tune, I was told, is called "The Delight." It had the same quality, the same soul expression, as though it were the language of the scene.

The sun was going down, and we were entering the port of Batavia.

My readers may know but little of Dutch India, and Batavia, its principal seaport.

Batavia is the capital of Dutch India, or the island empire of the Netherlands in the East Indies. It is situated on the river Jaccatra, near the sea. It is an old city and a new, the new arising out of the old. The vertical sun has made it a graveyard of Europeans; yet it still continues to be the emporium of the East, and has nearly an hundred thousand inhabitants.

If we consider the city to be connected with Buitezorg, the government depots, it is great indeed, and contains nearly a million inhabitants.

JAVA.

Java is the Cuba of the Indian Ocean. It is nearly seven hundred miles long. It is a volcanic island, and some of its peaks are twelve thousand feet in height.

Like most volcanic islands, it has the most luxuriant vegetation, very noxious animals, and gorgeous flowers. The interior is covered by dense forests of teak, and coffee plantations in the mellow light diversify the mountain-sides. Sago-palms shade the long valleys. Here live the rhinoceros and the blade tiger, and crocodiles infest the rank marshes; and some twenty kinds of deadly snakes are found, some of them of enormous size. Here the bird of Paradise sports amid flowers as gorgeous as its own plumage; and here the swallow exudes from its own mouth its waxy nest, the great delicacy of China.

The people live on rice, and make their money by exporting coffee and sugar.

Java is a colony, or province, of Holland, and the Dutch ships carry on its trade. These facts have been given or implied in the story of the "Flying Dutchwoman." I had received from that story a very correct impression of Java.

There was a quaint legend among old travellers and explorers that the island of Java formed the picture of a hog. "The figure of the island of Java," says an old chronicler, "resembles a hog couched on its four legs, with its head towards the Channel of Balaberao, and its hind legs to the mouth of the Straits of Sunda. The southern coast is his back."

The rival city of Batavia in the East Indies is Singapore, a port as magnificent and with a local population nearly as large. The Dutch Government had laid a telegraph line from Batavia to Singapore, — a distance of some six hundred miles, — and it was proposed to extend this line inland.

CHINESE DEVOURED BY MAN-EATING TIGERS.

Soon after my arrival I was given a place in the service of the East India Telegraph Company, which had agencies at the time both in Batavia and Singapore. In this service I passed twice between the two cities, and made two journeys inland.

If Ivory's influence had softened my heart toward animals in Florida, — and I am glad to say that it had, — the feeling was in a measure lost at Singapore. Stories of tigers, and of Chinese who had been devoured by man-eating tigers, filled the city, and I came to look upon harmless pussy but a tiger in miniature, a little tiger; and my gun began aimless service again in the bright Indian seas. I did not hunt tigers, — I would not have had the courage to do so; but I killed many harmless animals instead. Men are as cruel to animals in Batavia and Singapore as the fox-hunters of England or the buffalo-hunters on the American plains.

I had almost lost Ivory's influence at Singapore, when my feelings underwent a shock that recalled me to it again.

I was out one day with some English telegraphers and linemen, when I saw what seemed to me to be a strange bird swimming in a quiet and shaded place in the river. I raised my gun and fired.

There followed a scream, and a girl's form rose to the surface and came to the shore bleeding. She was a Malay, and her head was ornamented with feathers that had risen above the water as she had drifted under it.

No limbs were broken. She was taken in charge of her friends, who looked upon me with such indignation that I was glad to hurry back to the city.

But the sight of that bleeding arm long haunted me; and when it did so, Ivory's Hindu philosophy, that all life should be regarded as sacred, was impressed upon me.

The Javans, or Javanese, have some singular superstitions; among them, one that all familiar places are under the guardianship of spirits. The island is full of spiritualism.

Singapore is a rich city. In 1824 it was taken under the supervision of the East India Company by a treaty with the Sultan of Jabore. Its marts of wealth from that time began to increase. It

"AND YET THE MICE DO NOT LOVE THE CAT."

has nearly an hundred thousand inhabitants; its laws are those of Great Britain. It is a free port, and the seat of government for the Straits settlements.

Outside of the city the cocoanut, the pepper-vine, and sugar-cane abound. The country around used to be haunted by tigers. It has been estimated that some three hundred natives used to be killed by these beasts yearly.

"Here," said an Englishman to me, "mice are men, and the tiger is the cat."

"And yet," said another, "the mice do not like the cat, but call her cruel. *Hæc fabula docet*, etc."

In a former chapter we interpolated the story of the "Flying Dutchwoman." The story of the "Flying Dutchman" was the old legend of the Holland ships and traders in the bright Indian seas.

THE FLYING DUTCHMAN.

Many years ago, when the East Indies were regarded in all European countries as the treasure islands of the seas, there lived in Amsterdam, Holland, a Dutch sea-captain by the name of Vanderdecken. He possessed great physical strength and a spirit of daring; he had grown very rich by trading in the Dutch colonies in the Indies, and very proud too with his riches. He met and outrode many gales, and he came to regard himself as a man of destiny, to whose will all things were possible.

At this time there was a great Dutch city on the Straits of Sunda, now decayed, but once a golden treasure-house in the view of the sailors of the Netherlands. Vessels went out of Amsterdam empty, but returned from the Java Sea laden with fruits and treasures. In short, the sailor was looked upon as a sea king who sailed for the Java Sea.

Of course there was no Suez Canal at this time, and the burgomasters, as the mayors of the Dutch and Flemish towns were called, went around the far Cape of Good Hope in their voyages to gather the wealth of the Indian seas.

Vanderdecken was not a reverent man. He was proud of his defiance of religion and the Church.

One day the pious people of Amsterdam were pleased with the sight of a fine vessel in the harbor.

"When does she sail?" was asked.

"To-morrow," was answered by the sailors.

"To-morrow is Good Friday," said the people. "Some ships have sailed away on Friday, but they have all been lost. Such a thing as a ship sailing on Good Friday never was known. What will become of her?"

The sailors themselves looked frightened, but said, —

"We can trust our captain for that."

"VESSELS WENT OUT OF AMSTERDAM EMPTY."

"Who is your captain?"
"Vanderdecken."
"Where is the ship bound for?"

"A STRANGE FORM APPEARED ON THE DECK."

"The Java seas."

The next day was Good Friday. Bells filled the April air, — solemn bells, — and while they were ringing, the sails of the ship arose, and the ship passed down the harbor and into the sea.

Wondering eyes watched her. "What will become of her? What will become of her?" asked all the people. Many answered, "She never will return."

The Dutch at this time controlled the wonderland of Borneo, as to-day. The city on the Javan Sea to which their ships went for treasure was called Bantam. This city declined on the rise of Batavia.

Vanderdecken had a prosperous voyage until he reached the Cape of Good Hope, when the ship encountered a most furious gale. The weather was so fierce that the sailors began to fear that evil spirits possessed the air. Days passed, and the gale continued. The ship made no progress, but was tossed about like a bubble.

A week passed, and still the winds lashed the waters. The ship was driven hither and thither, and her bare cordage shrieked in the ceaseless winds.

The sailors came to Vanderdecken, and asked, "What does this mean?"

"Mr. Captain," said one, "you cannot defy God, — the heavens are against us. Remember Good Friday."

At this Vanderdecken grew very angry with winds, with the sailors, and with fate.

"Howl on!" he said to the wild sky and white waves. "Blow! beat! I will double the Cape if I have to sail to all eternity. Howl! blow! beat!"

A darkness came over the sea, and a strange form appeared on the deck of the ship and stood by the Captain.

"I have heard your vow," said the mysterious figure. "You shall sail on forever."

The word "forever" struck terror even to the proud heart of Vanderdecken.

"Who are you?"

"I raised the storm."

"The Evil One?"

"So men call me."

"I am to sail on forever?"

"Yes, forever."

"And never come to port?"

"Never."

"But will you not grant me some condition of release?"

"No."

"Not one?"

"Yes, one," said the dark figure with a sneer; "if you will find one heart in the world that is always true, I will release you. But that will never, never release you, for such a heart never yet was found."

"Not in women?"

"Man nor woman."

"But how can I find such a heart unless I can go into port?"

"You may go into port once in seven years, under the spell."

The air grew darker.

"Sail on forever!" said the figure. The darkness deepened, and he was gone.

Time went on, and the ship was driven hither and thither from one sea to another, by gale upon gale. The sails turned red like blood, and the masts turned black. The sailors grew white and thin, and the face of Vanderdecken came to wear a look of unutterable sorrow and remorse.

Sometimes the fated Captain would meet a ship and try to send letters back to Holland; but the ships that received his letters never came to port. His ship became the terror of sailors, and no vessel that met him would take letters from him.

Every seven years he would enter some port, under the spell, in search of one true heart. But under the spell he would have to sail away again, each time more hopeless and in deeper sorrow.

So a hundred or more years passed; and his ship, like a skeleton, was tossed about by the gales.

The ships of the sea all shunned him. It was regarded as an evil omen so much as to see the "Flying Dutchman," as the ship of Vanderdecken came to be called.

His relatives died, and his friends, — all whom he had loved. "Oh that I might forget the past," he would say, — "the faces of those who loved me, my evil influence, and my evil deeds!"

A sailor came to him one day, and said, —

"I will tell you a secret."

"What?"

"How to find a true heart and get released."

"That would make you a friend to me, indeed. How?"

"Truth finds its own. Repent, and carry a true heart yourself, and you will find another true heart. Do not the same elements find each other?"

There came over Vanderdecken a great change.

"How will any one know that my own heart is true?" he asked one day of the sailor.

"The soul has its atmospheres and influences that are unseen. Space does not bound them. Like thought finds like thought, and like feeling like feeling, across the world. We meet people in strange places whom we have met

"HE WOULD HAVE TO SAIL AWAY AGAIN."

in the soul atmospheres before, and we know them and they know us, though we have never seen each other."

"You talk like a man of the world, and not like a doomed wanderer of the sea."

The ship with her red sails and black masts was driven away from the hot seas towards the cold coasts of Norway. Seven years since he had learned the secret of being true, to find in others a true heart, had passed, and he again set foot upon the land.

In the old Norwegian seaport there lived a sea-captain named Daland. He had a beautiful daughter, whose name was Senta. The home of this merchant-captain had been enriched with works of art from many lands, and among the pictures in the room of his beautiful daughter was a portrait of the Flying Dutchman.

The face in the picture was one of great sadness, as representing a penitent and broken spirit, and about the time of Vanderdecken's new purpose in life, which he may be supposed to have adopted. The picture began to make a strange impression upon the beautiful Senta.

"Tell me about the Dutchman," she said one day to her father, soon after he had come into port.

"He is doomed to sail forever."

"Is there no hope for him?"

"None, unless he can find a true heart to love him."

"I love him, and I wish I could release him."

"But you have not a true heart."

"Why?"

"No one has."

"Did you ever know me to be untrue?"

"No."

"A heart governed in all things by a sense of right cannot be untrue."

"But how about your lover, young Eric?"

"He may love me, but I only respect him. I do not return his love, and I have told him so, although it has cost me nights of pain. Is not that being true?"

"And cruel?"

"No. Eric has worth, but it is not destined for me. I have told him the truth."

Vanderdecken, on entering the Norwegian port, found another ship there which had just come in from the seas. It was Daland's. The two captains made each other's acquaintance, and Daland invited Vanderdecken to share the hospitalities of his home.

So far in the story we have followed the old sailor's legend and Heine's variations and the old London play, and made some colorings of our own; we will now follow Wagner, which seems destined to become the popular evolution of the story.

At the time that Vanderdecken enters the Norwegian port, Wagner's musical version of the story represents Senta as spinning among her maidens and singing to them the following song, —

"HE IS DOOMED TO SAIL FOREVER."

"Yo-ho-ho! Yo-ho-ho-ho! Yo-ho-ho! Yo-ho!
A ship the restless ocean sweeps;
Blood-red her sails, and black her masts;
Her spectral captain never sleeps,
But watchful glances round him casts.
Hui! The wind is shrill! Yo-ho-he! Yo-ho-he!
Hui! The wind is shrill! Yo-ho-he! Yo-ho-he!
Hui! Like an arrow he flies, without aim, without rest, without end.
Yet this the spectral man from his lifelong curse may deliver,
Find he a maiden, faithful and true, to love him forever.
Ah! mightest thou, spectral seaman, but find her!
Pray ye, that heaven may soon
At his need grant him this boon.

"Against a tempest's utmost wrath,
Around a cape he once would sail;
He cursed and swore a foolish oath:
'Befall what may, I will prevail!'
Hui! And Satan heard! Yo-ho-he!
Hui! He marked his word,
And condemned him to sail on the sea, without aim, without end.
Yet this the wretched man from his lifelong curse may deliver,
Would but an angel show him the way his bondage to sever.
Ah! mightest thou, spectral seaman, but find it!
Pray ye that heaven may soon
At his need grant him this boon! .
He lands at every seven years' end;
A wife to seek, he wanders round;
But wheresoe'er he bends
For him no faithful wife is found.
Hui! 'Unfurl the sails!' Yo-ho-he!
Hui! 'The anchor weighed!' Yo-ho-he!
Hui! 'Faithless love, faithless troth!
To the sea, without aim, without end!'"

While the beautiful Senta was singing this song, Eric, her lover, saw her father's sail coming into port, and hastened to her to tell her the joyful news. She awaited her father with a thrill of unusual expectation and joy. She saw him approach the house, when, lo! a stranger came with him.

But Eric, before Daland's arrival, has pressed his suit and asked Senta for her heart. She pointed to the face of the Flying Dutchman on the wall, when Eric told her of a dream that he has had, and of his heart's sorrow.

The stranger was the Flying Dutchman; and the wanderer of the seas knew the beautiful maiden, and she knew him, although they had never met before. Vanderdecken, in Wagner's version of the story, is made to say, —

> "Like to a vision, seen in days long by-gone,
> This maiden's face and form appear;
> What I have sought thro' countless years of sorrow
> Am I at last beholding here."

The Flying Dutchman avowed his love for Senta, and she announced herself to be his deliverer. Both were happy.

But amid the happiness and hope Eric came back to plead once more with the maiden. The interview was one of agony, and in the midst of it Vanderdecken chanced to come upon the scene. Seeing the distress of the two, he believed that Senta was untrue to him, and that he was destined again to drift over the seas.

With a crushed heart, he ordered his ship to sea again, and the red sails went out with the tide.

When Senta found that he was sailing, she attempted to follow him. The last scene is like that of Dido and Æneas. Senta ascended a high rock, and watched the disappearing red sails.

"I will die true to him," she said, and plunged into the sea.

The spell was broken. The phantom ship went down with a thunder crash, and the sailors drifted upon the sea. The dying Captain was borne on the tide into the arms of the dying Senta, and their souls entered together the portals of immortal hope.

This is the version of the story that we like the best. "Blackwood's Magazine" for 1821 has a very sensational story of a ship meeting the "Flying Dutchman;" and the story is made very real in Marryatt's "Phantom Ship."

The evolution of the story, like that of Faust, given in another volume, finally saves the Dutchman from his eternal wanderings, which is a very kind and pleasing end to all evolutionary stories.

While at Batavia, I met an agent of the International Postal Union, who accompanied me to Singapore on one of my trips, and who offered me a new situation in a company of which I had never so

"LIKE TO A VISION SEEN IN DAYS LONG BY-GONE."

much as heard before, yet by whose services I, in common with most Americans, had profited.

THE INTERNATIONAL POSTAL UNION was its name. The Company was formed in Paris in 1863, when delegates met for the purpose from all European States, from the United States, and other parts of the world. The Congress recommended the optional payment of foreign letters, and among other things improvement in routes of transit in new postal countries. In 1874 another Congress met for the same purpose at Berne, with representatives of 350,000 people. Under this Congress's influence the uniform rate of five cents per half-ounce for foreign letters was established throughout the civilized world. At the close of this Congress Dr. Stephen, of Prussia, a leading delegate, said:

"You enter upon one of the most important fields of action in the intercourse of nations; you are doing a work of universal peace."

Another Postal Congress met at Lisbon in 1885.

Among the curious things discussed here, was to whom a letter belongs during transit. In Great Britain it belongs to the Queen; in India, to the owner, and it may be recalled by him; in Italy and Spain, to the person addressed, as also in Canada.

My friend was employed, under the direction of a committee of the International Postal Union, in the improvement of Postal Routes in the East. He offered me a position to travel with him to Burmah, and thence inland at a salary largely in advance from that I was receiving from the East Indian Telegraph Company.

I accepted the position; and we went to Bangkok together on especial business there, where I again met Ivory.

CHAPTER XV.

BANGKOK AGAIN.

ON returning to Bangkok I found Ivory's mind still occupied with the one subject on which I had heard him speak so often.

"If I could be given a mission," he said, "it would be to establish Societies for the Prevention of Cruelty to Animals in other parts of the world."

"What do you mean by other parts of the world?" I asked.

"Other than Buddhist countries. Think of it! fifty millions of animals are slaughtered yearly for food, and many millions more for sport; and yet the people live the longest and are the happiest and have the fewest diseases, who do not eat animal food at all."

"So you are about to turn Buddhist and a vegetarian?" I said, with a smile.

His father, who was present, entered into the spirit of my reproachful remark.

"Ivory is so touched by what he regards cruelty to animals in other parts of the world, that he fails to see the cruelty of superstition to men and women and children in this part of the world. Here is Bangkok, a paradise of beauty, full of the most inhuman practices growing out of old superstition, and only Christianity can remove these evils; yet he is giving his heart and thoughts merely to the animal kingdom, and that as found in Christian countries. Yesterday he wrote a letter to a friend in Boston, and sent a pound in behalf of a Coachmen's Humane Association, which is about to be formed in that city of many ideas. I reproved him, for I felt that his money was needed here to enlighten the suffering poor and relieve them from idolatrous habits that hold them as if in chains. Why, one day when I was in Laos, I saw a scorpion suddenly bite an innocent child,

"MANY MILLIONS MORE FOR SPORT."

and the mother of the child brush the scorpion gently away with a stick. The child went into convulsions and died; and the mother, amid her lamentations, expressed a wish that the scorpion might be reborn in the form of some higher animal. To her it was the sin of some dead ancestor that made the scorpion a scorpion."

"But, father, each one is born for some special good work in the world. It is your call to help these poor people into a better life, and to preach the light of the Gospel. But there is another impulse in me; ought I not to follow my own heart in the best work that moves it?"

"I do not know, Ivory; but it seems to me that one should do the work of humanity first."

"But the Hebrew Law gives regarded justice to the animal world as one of the works of humanity. Think of the bird's-nest commandment, and the Hebrew injunction that the ox should not be muzzled when treading out the grain."

Ivory's father looked puzzled. A telegrapher was with us, and he remarked laughingly,—

"Ivory will never be likely to harm any very large animal, unless his looks belie him. His legs would do him good service if he were to meet any animal larger than a cat."

"Why do you say that?" asked Ivory's father.

"Why? Because I've seen him run from a jackal."

"I think the boy in the face of actual danger would develop more courage than you give him credit for. In the words of an American poet, 'The tenderest are the bravest,' and 'The loving are the daring.'"

Siam and Laos, like the land of Sind, are filled with beautiful stories of the friendships of men and animals. One charming feature of these stories is that the animals are supposed to possess instincts that make them wiser than men.

THE BLIND MAN, THE DEAF MAN, AND THEIR FRIEND THE DONKEY.

There was once a Blind Man.

And a Deaf Man.

Said the Deaf Man to the Blind Man, "Let us be friends. I will be eyes for you, and you shall be ears for me."

"AN IDOLATROUS HABIT."

So they adopted each other as brothers, and both now had eyes and ears. They went to a dance together.

Said the Blind Man, "The music is good, but the dancing is poor."

Said the Deaf Man, "The dancing is good, but the music is poor."

When they rested and described what one had heard and the other had seen, they agreed that both the music and the dancing were good.

It is good to have friends.

The two started on a journey. On their way they met a forlorn Donkey.

"It is good to have friends," said the Deaf Man. "Here is a poor outcast Donkey; let us take him along, it may be he will do us good. It always pays to be friendly."

So the three became friends.

They came to an ant-hill.

Said the Deaf Man, "Here are some wonderful ants, the largest that I ever saw. Let us take some of them along with us to show to the friends we meet."

"Very well," said the Blind Man.

So the Deaf Man put some of the ants into a silver snuff-box, and the three continued on their journey.

There arose a fearful storm.

"THEY MET A FORLORN DONKEY."

"The lightning is dreadful," said the Deaf Man.

"The thunder is awful," said the Blind Man.

"Where shall we go?" said both.

There rose before them the shadow as of a mighty temple. The Deaf Man saw it.

"There is a great building close at hand," said the Deaf Man.

"Let us go in," said the Blind Man.

And the Donkey did not say nay; so the three went into the grand building out of the rain.

Now, the building was not a temple, but the palace of a Rakshas.

A Rakshas is a monster, with an evil spirit, that feeds upon men.

Hardly had the three friendly travellers got inside the palace and shut the door, when the Rakshas came home and hurried to the door to get away from the storm.

To his surprise he found the door fastened.

"Ho, ho!" he said. "Who is there?"

"Ho, ho!" said the Blind Man. "Who is *there?*"

"The Rakshas."

Then he roared like thunder; for the Rakshases have terrible voices.

The Deaf Man peeped through the window, and began to tremble when he saw the Rakshas. But the Blind Man was very brave.

"Ho, ho!" again cried the Evil Spirit. "Let me into my house at once. Let me in, I say."

Then he roared again. But the Deaf Man did not hear him.

Then said the Blind Man, "Go away, and leave us alone. I do not think that you know who I am."

"Who are you?" roared the Rakshas.

"I am a Bakshas."

"A Bakshas! What is that?"

"It is something very terrible."

"Nonsense! There is no such thing as a Bakshas."

Nor was there.

"Let me see you," said the Rakshas. "You are deceiving me."

"What shall we do?" said the Blind Man.

"What *shall* we do?" said the Deaf Man.

"I have it," said the Deaf Man. Show him the head of the Donkey. How good it is to have a friend! Every friend helps sometime or somewhere."

So the Deaf Man opened the window a little, and pushed the Donkey up to it, and caused the animal to show his head.

"Heavens and earth!" said the Rakshas. "A Bakshas is awful, indeed."

"Awful, indeed," said the Blind Man.

"Does a Bakshas roar like a Rakshas?" asked the monster.

"Yes," said the Blind Man; "his voice chills all who hear it. The second time he roars men drop dead."

"Let me hear you roar once," said the Rakshas.

The Deaf Man here took out the silver snuff-box of ants, and put an ant into the ear of the Donkey.

"Eh augh! eh augh! eh augh! augh! augh!" roared the Donkey.

"Run," said the Blind Man, "or he will roar again."

"Heavens and earth!" said the Rakshas, beginning to run with his fingers in his ears.

The three spent the night in the palace. In the morning the Blind Man said to the Deaf Man, "What do you see?"

"The palace is full of gold."

"NOW THE BUILDING WAS NOT A TEMPLE, BUT THE PALACE OF A BAKSHAS."

"Load the Donkey with it."

So the two loaded the Donkey with as much gold as he could carry and started for home.

The three lived happily together for many years, each helping the others.

It is good to have friends.

THE IDOL-MAKER'S DAUGHTER.

MRS. LEONOWENS, IN THE "YOUTH'S COMPANION," BY PERMISSION.

After that of the royal barber, who is privileged to shave, consequently touch, the heads of kings and princes, the most honorable profession in Siam is that of an idol-maker.

This latter profession is held in superstitious reverence. Very few young persons embrace it, because of a dread of incurring the vengeance of the gods they manufacture, should they at any time happen to disgrace by the smallest fault their holy profession.

In order to embrace the profession of making idols for the temples of Siam, three things are requisite. The man must know the three most sacred books of the Buddhists. He must have entered the priesthood at some period of his life. He must be an unmarried man at the time of undertaking the work, and must remain unmarried so long as he continues to manufacture idols.

In addition to these requirements, if the first idol he moulds and puts into the kiln to bake should have any crack in it when it is taken out,— and this often happens from the heat of the kiln into which the image is put to bake,— the man must not enter the profession, for this is regarded as a sign of the displeasure of the gods against him.

Taking these things into consideration, the profession is entered under many difficulties, and is therefore generally taken up by old men, widowers, ex-priests, or perhaps some devotee, who has become disgusted with life, and takes refuge in this occupation as a meritorious one, that will give admittance into another and better life after death.

With this brief explanation, I must introduce my young readers to Phra Khoon Visatt, the royal idol-maker of Bangkok, and his daughter Champoo.

His house, or workshop, was situated immediately behind our home in Bangkok, so that he was my next-door neighbor. It was a large circular shed, walled all round with a mud-plastered bamboo fence, and open to the sky. A brick kiln stood in the middle of it, and two or three covered partitions, that served him for his humble sleeping-room and kitchen. Here Phra Khoon

Visatt lived and worked alone, modelling and baking clay idols without number, presenting them to the king for his innumerable temples, refusing all reward, in the hope of reaping a rich one in the life to come.

He was a widower with one daughter. As he was too poor to clothe and feed her, she lived with her uncle, in a rather large and pretentious dwelling close by. She visited her father every day, and sometimes cooked his food for him, when he happened to be sick, or was too weary to do it for himself. And so far as I could see, there seemed to be deep affection in the heart of this lonely old maker of idols for his gay and light-headed daughter.

I do not remember the precise date of the first awakening of my interest in my strange pagan neighbor. I had watched him for a long time from my upper veranda. From that position I could look down into his workshop, and see him modelling the wet clay. There, day after day, he worked, fashioning from the plastic material the same eternal figure of the Buddha, — the likeness of a stolid, indifferent-looking man, in a sitting posture, his eyes closed, his legs crossed, and his hands resting calmly upon each knee. Sometimes I saw him at prayer, kneeling in his workshop before his newly formed idol, his pale, haggard face turned up to the blue sky,

IDOL OF THE GOD OF WISDOM.

while he implored his god to be beneficent to him, and not crack the moment he put it in the kiln to bake.

Sometimes his daughter would come into his workshop unannounced. Finding him on his knees, she would bend down for a few minutes beside him. Then she would jump up and betake herself to all kinds of merry-making.

Round and round the shed she would dance, in the presence of the solemn idols that were waiting their turn to be baked, singing funny songs. Taking cards from her vest, she would throw them down on the ground and perform certain tricks which seemed to give her infinite satisfaction, for she would laugh loudly over them. This light-headedness the idol-maker seemed to permit rather than to enjoy.

But I noticed that his face brightened when she was by, that his eyes lingered fondly over her face, and it was always full of the tenderest affection.

It was on a bright Christmas day that I carried my neighbor, Phra Khoon Visatt, a little present for his gay young daughter. It consisted of a red cotton

"THE SAME ETERNAL FIGURE OF BUDDHA."

handkerchief, of Malay manufacture, which the Siamese women are very fond of holding in their hands when dressed in holiday attire, and which I thought would please the father's heart more than any gift for himself.

Thus it happened that on that memorable day, sacred to us as the anniversary of our dear Saviour's birth, the 25th of December, 1864, I stood for the first time before the door of the idol-maker's workshop, with the little gift in my hand, and knocked for admittance.

In an instant the door was opened, and I stood face to face with my neighbor. He was a pale, emaciated-looking man, with sunken cheeks and deep-set eyes. He seemed almost ready to drop into the grave, but, supporting himself against the open door, smiled kindly upon me, and inquired my business with him.

"Business I have none," said I; "but I have brought you a little present for the pretty, gay young woman who visits you every day. This is my great day, the day on which my Divine teacher was born, and it is our custom to show our love for Him by making little gifts to our friends; and as you are my next-door neighbor, you must let me include you too among my friends."

It was a long speech for me to make in Siamese, but he seemed to understand me fully. He took the little package which I held out to him, smiling at me and looking wistfully into my face with his deep-sunken eyes, as if he hardly knew what to say.

At length he said very slowly, and with some hesitation, "I am very sorry at my heart because I cannot ask you into my workshop. But this is a sacred place, and you have shoes on your feet, and altogether I am afraid lest my god would be offended with me, and then I would lose all the merit I have been making these many years. But I thank you for your gift, very, very much in his name, and in my dear daughter Champoo's too."

He looked anxiously at me after saying this, fearing lest I should be offended, adding, "I never allow any one but my daughter to come in here, lest I should incur the anger of my god in any way."

I could not tell him that he was right, but I said, "I hope you will soon be better, and if I can do anything for you, let me know, because it will give me pleasure to do it;" and I came home again.

In the afternoon of the same day, as I was seated in my veranda, I saw Champoo enter the workshop, and I had the curiosity to watch father and daughter.

The idol-maker was in the very act of moulding one of his images on a long plank or board. His hands were smeared with clay.

The daughter entered and sat down beside him, looking rather graver and quieter than usual. After a little while he put away his work, washed his hands, and with a smile on his face drew from his pocket my little gift, and held it up before her.

The girl gave a quick, glad cry, snatched it out of his hand with one

"BOTH GIRLS WERE LAUGHING AND SHRIEKING, AND MAKING MERRY OVER THEIR WORK."

sudden pull, and without giving him time, as it seemed to me, to say a single word, bounded out of the workshop with it.

I followed her with my eyes as far as I could see her. Away she flew, fluttering the gay handkerchief before her, till she entered her uncle's house and passed from my sight.

I turned to look at the poor, lone idol-maker. He was at work again, moulding the plastic clay into the same old form; and I could not tell whether he resented his daughter's conduct, or whether he was so accustomed to such acts from her that he did not heed them.

Whatever he may have felt, I must confess that there arose great pity in my heart for the lonely old man, mingled with a painful sense of my own inability to do anything to make his life any happier or better.

One Sunday morning, about six weeks more or less after this event, I heard a piercing cry issuing from the workshop. The voice was that of a young girl, shrieking out the words, —

"Phoa, phoa, phut chau thort! phut chau thort!" (Father, father, please speak to me! please speak to me!)

I rushed to my place of outlook in the upper veranda. The poor idol-maker was stretched on the floor. His daughter was holding his head, gazing wildly into his face, and uttering every now and then the piercing cries I had heard.

He was evidently in a fainting-fit. I rushed to my closet, drew out from it a bottle of camphor, some wine and cologne, ran downstairs, and round the yard to the workshop, and was soon kneeling beside the fainting man.

There he lay on the bare ground, his face turned up to the sky, his eyes fixed, his hands clasped as if in prayer or supplication, at the feet of a great clay idol of Buddha, which must have been recently drawn out of the kiln, and which was cracked through and through from head to foot.

Crushed by the sight of what he considered his god's displeasure, feeling that he had forfeited all his years of patient, unremitting labor, and worn out at the same time with his fasting and generally failing health, he had fallen into the swoon in which his daughter found him.

His heart still throbbed, and there was a faint gurgling sound in his throat. I sat down beside him, and rubbed the camphor to his hands and feet, poured wine down his throat, applied the camphor-bottle to his nostrils. It was all in vain. There on the very spot where Phra Rhoon Visatt had sat and worked and prayed and moulded, year in and year out, clay images of his god, some to be overlaid with gold, others with silver, — there he gave up the last struggling breath of his poor frail body. In twenty minutes after I had entered the workshop, he was dead.

When this sad fact dawned upon his daughter's mind, she put her mouth to his deaf ears, and began to shout to the soul who once so gladly heard her voice through them, —

"Phoa, pi savang nah! Phoa, pi savang nah!" (Father, be sure and go to heaven! Father, be sure and go to heaven!)

I vainly tried to comfort the poor girl; but as some strangers had now entered the workshop, attracted by her cries, I rose and left, feeling sad and sorrowful enough that there was nothing more to be done. After breakfast, I once more looked down into the workshop, and saw there a sight which I shall never forget.

The dead man was lying just where he had died. The strangers, whoever they were, had all gone, and Champoo and a slave girl were scraping the clay from the board on which the idol-maker moulded his images. A long earth-worm had crawled out of the clay, and both girls were laughing and shrieking, and making merry over their work.

I could hardly believe my senses. At last they cleansed the board, and laid a mat on it; and, taking up the dead man, Champoo holding his head, and the slave girl his feet, they lifted him as easily as if he were a child, and laid him on it.

Then they both went off. Presently they returned, bringing with them some palm-branches and some oleander flowers to deck his bier. This done, to my utter surprise, once more Champoo sat down beside him and began to howl and cry, striking her breast and screaming, —

"Oh, my father, my father! why did you die?"

I did not know what to make of the girl, at one time so loving and tender, and at another so hard and heartless.

That very afternoon, my maid announced some Siamese ladies as visitors. Before I had time to decline seeing them, in walked Champoo, with three other girls. They bore a tray, upon which was some fruit sent in by her uncle.

This she handed to me, and said, "Lady, will you please give me a long piece of muslin to wrap round my father's body when he is carried to be burned? It was his wish that no one should touch him after death but me, and I want to do everything nicely."

I was just in the act of undressing to take my afternoon bath, and had deposited my rings in a little tray on my toilet-table, where I left her standing, and turned to seek the muslin she needed in a closet adjoining.

She was delighted with my gift. I gave her a long strip, for she wished to

"WE WALKED BY THE CANAL."

have some part of it placed over her dead father's face, so that the flies might not alight on it as it was being carried to the cremation grounds. Then she went away.

That evening, as the men came to carry off the poor idol-maker's body to be burned, I and my boy followed it. There were a few mourners, the chief among whom was Champoo, howling, throwing dust over her head, and beating her breast.

When we arrived at the cremation grounds, they laid the dead body on a low wood pyre. Two Buddhist priests poured some oil over it, chanting funereal dirges all the while. Then Champoo was handed a torchlight. With it she ignited the wood; and in a few minutes the whole pyre was blazing, crackling, and consuming the last remains of that poor hopeless maker of idols.

I left them at their fiery work, and returned home sickened and dispirited. It was already evening. The sun had set in great beauty. Not a sound was heard; not an object was moving anywhere.

My boy and I passed on to the little canal that ran behind our house. The plumes of the palm-trees hung still and motionless, as if mourning for the departure of the bright god of day; and I sorrowed, almost unconsciously, for my dead neighbor.

We walked by the canal, and found some distraction in watching the gliding canoes. Suddenly feeling my hand, my boy said, " Mamma, where are your rings? "

" I must have forgotten to put them on, Louis," said I. " They are on my toilet-table."

When we returned home, I went to my table. My rings were not on it. Neither could I find them in the room, though I remembered taking them off that very afternoon in the presence of Champoo.

I searched, questioned my servants, but in vain. Every one declared that no person could have taken them but one of the girls who had entered my chamber that day. I did not know what to think; but, to satisfy my servants, I sent one of them, accompanied by my boy, to inquire if Champoo had taken the rings, and if so to beg of her to return them.

In a short space of time Champoo, followed by my son and servant, stood before me. She was in a wild state of excitement. She said, " Oh, lady, how can you have the heart to accuse me of taking your rings, when you must have lost them yourself? "

" I do not accuse you, Champoo," said I, very gently. " I do not know what to think. My servants are honest. No persons have entered the house to-day save you and your slaves. Perhaps one of them may have taken the rings."

"No, indeed," said Champoo, looking highly offended, and making me feel very guilty because of my seeming unjust suspicions; "my slaves are no thieves! You have lost them yourself!" and she marched up and down the room.

Just then we heard the click of something falling on the marble floor; and there, right in front of me, lay one of my missing rings. I stooped and picked it up.

"That is the way," said the girl, taking another turn, "that you drop your things around."

Presently another click on the polished floor, and my second ring was seen and picked up. After this, Champoo turned to go away. I was so pained and surprised that I had lost all power of speech. Just then my boy ran up to me and said, —

"Mamma, don't you see that the other ring is in her closed hand? Make her give it up!"

Hardly knowing what I was doing, I went up to Champoo, and, taking her closed hand in mine, was going to remonstrate with her; but before I could say a word, she opened her palm, and there was my third missing ring lying in it.

I was so shocked, thinking of her lately dead father, that I could not speak. Finally, I stammered, "Cham — Champoo, did you — did you take those rings from my table, or was it one of your slaves who did it?"

"Why," said Champoo, laughing merrily, "I took them under your very nose, and you were such a goose you did not see me doing it!"

With that she handed me the ring, and, jerking herself away from my grasp, left me more puzzled and grieved than I can well express.

But after a day or two had passed, I remembered that this habit of pilfering was the chief failing of the Siamese. So I determined to treat Champoo just the same as ever, if she should need my help and come to me for it.

Full eighteen months passed. In that time I had often thought of Champoo, and wondered where she was. One afternoon I thought I saw a young woman coming towards my house. She looked like Champoo. There was a baby in her arms. I looked again, and found that it was my wayward friend, the idol-maker's daughter.

When she saw me smiling at her from the dining-room in which I was seated, she ran up to me, and, putting the baby in my arms, fell down at my feet, took hold of them, and burst into a loud passion of tears and sobs, which brought the tears to my eyes.

Stooping over her, I lifted her up, wiped her eyes, told her how glad I was to see her, and inquired the nature of her new trouble.

"Oh, lady," said Champoo, still sobbing and speaking in spite of them, " I have no more troubles, I am very happy. I am married to a very good man, who loved my poor father very much, and I am growing good too. My baby is making me good, he is so dear and precious. I wanted to come and tell you that I am sorry, oh, so sorry, that I did not do more for my poor, kind father!"

Here she burst into fresh loud sobs. In a moment she said, "Now that I am a mother, and look into my little baby's face, I know, alas! how my poor father loved me, and how he must have cared for me. My mother died the day after I was born, and he was both father and mother to me, until he began to work for the future life in making those idols. I have been very wicked. But oh, please love me a little, and help me to be good!"

With Champoo's arms round my neck, and her little boy in my lap, we made a new promise of friendship, which we kept to the day of my leaving Bangkok, and which I believe still binds her to me, though we are separated by wide seas, and wider customs and religions.

Still she was changed into a good, tender, and gentle mother and wife, always doing her duty, and trying, as she said, "to grow good." Her better nature had triumphed at last in the clear light of a mother's love and its sweet responsibilities.

TO MAULMAIN.

My new duties led me to go next to Maulmain. Ivory went with me. We journeyed with a party of telegraphers and railroad section men, going up the Meinam, and crossing the mountains, — a delightful journey through a wonderland of primitive races, interesting animals, gay birds, and beautiful flowers.

The kingdom of Siam stretches from about the fourth to the twentieth degree of latitude, and is about twelve hundred miles long, scarcely more than the railway journey of a single day in English lands.

The Meinam is the great highway of the kingdom. The great plain through which the river flows is overgrown with jungle and forest. A mountain wall separates Siam from Burmah.

In the western mountains are the Karen tribes, among whom

American missionaries have labored with the greatest success. The Karens are a mild, intelligent people, susceptible to good influences and having many wonderful traditions. In the northern countries of Siam are the Laos people, also amiable and thoughtful, but very superstitious. Among them every house, garden, or household tree has its

"IN THE FALL THE RIVER OVERFLOWS ITS BANKS."

guardian spirit and to keep these spirits pleased and kindly is one of the principal concerns of the people.

In the fall the river overflows its banks. Then used to occur one of the most splendid festivals of Siam. When the river had risen for a certain time, the King would command an hundred Buddhist priests to go out on the water in grand barges of state, and command the waters to subside. The waters always obeyed the priests after more or less delay, just as the eclipse of the sun has always disappeared on the beating of Chinese gongs.

Our boat drifted away from the floating bazaars, palmy gardens, and golden wats or pagodas; and we found ourselves on the calm waters of the Meinam, leaving the scenes of the Siam of the present for those of the dead Siam of the past. We took with us our bread and provisions. The air glimmered with temples or wats, as the boat slowly drifted along. Our first anchorage was at Kanburee. Our trip lasted about fifteen days, nearly equally divided between boats and elephant riding.

Our journey on the elephants was through silent forests of cool bamboos. Families of monkeys were everywhere to be seen; and as we approached the Karen country, we saw many lovely gardens.

My first ride on an elephant seemed to me much like sailing on a heavy sea. It made me sick. After a time I became used to it, and

THE DRIVER SAT ON THE HEAD OF THE ELEPHANT.

liked the disposition of each friendly animal that I mounted. The elephant driver sat on the head of the animal, and assisted him in clearing away the bamboos in the thick forests.

We arrived at Maulmain early in December, and found the city greatly excited over an expected raid of the Decoits.

The Decoits are the bandits of Burmah. They are supposed to be countenanced by the Government, and to gain and hold the royal favor by paying high taxes into the royal treasury. They rally to the King in time of war.

The Decoits roam the country in armed bands, and plunder and kill whomsoever they will. Some of their crimes are most awful and cruel, among them the burning of helpless people who are unable to escape from a house or village during an attack. These victims are often old people, invalids, and children.

As the Decoits oppose the English rule, they have acquired a certain reputation for patriotism. In reality, they are nothing but robbers.

From Maulmain we journeyed on a boat towards Rangoon.

The country was so flat in some parts of the way that it seemed hard to tell which was the water or which was the land.

We were now on the Irrawaddy.

At last a dome glimmered in the sun. It looked like the State House dome from Boston harbor. A Burmese on the boat saw it, and fell upon his knees and began counting his beads.

At every bead which he told he uttered a sentence in a tone of the deepest sadness.

"What does he say?" I asked.

"'Vanity, misery, forgetfulness,' as near as I can translate it," said Ivory; "he means that the world is full of vanity and misery, and that he longs for forgetfulness. It is his prayer for the bliss of annihilation. The Burmese prayer is for non-existence."

Over and over it was repeated, — "Vanity, misery, oblivion."

The dome grew brighter, like a sun. I watched it grow and glow, while still sounded in my ears, "Vanity, misery, oblivion."

Rangoon is a city of nearly one hundred thousand inhabitants, among whom are some two thousand Christians. It is the stronghold of Buddhism, — a city of pagodas and temples and images

A PAGODA IN THE LAOS.

The temple which we had seen was the Golden Dragon, the foundation of which is said to have been laid twenty-three hundred years ago. It is a mountain of masonry. The whole stupendous pyramid seems to be overlaid with gold. The temple is regarded as especially sacred from the fact that it claims to contain eight hairs from the head of Gautama.

The country around Rangoon was, like Maulmain, in a state of excitement over the uprising of the Decoits. This was a cause of anxiety to us, as Ivory and two linemen were commissioned to travel inland from the city, and their journey would take them through some very dangerous localities.

I advised the party not to go; but Ivory merely said, —

"We have accepted the work; now let us do our duty."

I still urged delay.

"I have no fear," said Ivory.

"No fear of what?" said I.

"Of anything but wrong-doing."

"But if what we hear be true, you will expose yourself to death."

"I do not fear death," said Ivory.

"You long perhaps, like the Buddhist, for forgetfulness."

"No," said he, thoughtfully; "my trust is in Him who came to this earth, not to teach oblivion, but that men might have life, and have it more abundantly."

These were the last words that I ever heard Ivory utter. In a few hours after, he left Rangoon, and with a party of linemen went into the interior.

I was now indeed in the Antipodes. I began to feel at home. I had only to go down eight thousand miles, and I would be in America.

The following narrative is abridged from a missionary article by Rev. W. Bushell, of Maooben, and originally appeared in the "Baptist Missionary Magazine," October, 1882 (Boston).

TRIAL BY THE WATER-SPIRITS.

Leaving Maulmain on Dec. 5, 1881, we reached Zimmay on Jan. 10, 1882. We were fortunate in our time of arrival, as the city was just then much interested in a trial which was occupying the rulers.

Among the Laos people, when a man brings a civil case before the ordinary judge or magistrate, and is dissatisfied with the decision, he can appeal to the court of the chief and have it retried. Should he still be dissatisfied, by paying a heavy fee (a certain percentage of the amount at stake) he can appeal to the court of the Water-Spirits. This is the supreme court of the Laos tribe, and from its decision there is no appeal. The good spirits are supposed to assist the one who has the most righteous cause. Therefore, having once given its voice, there is no higher tribunal to which an appeal can be made; the question is settled forever.

The appeals to this court are not very numerous; because, in addition to the large fee each side has to pay into the hands of the chief before the case is tried, litigants are deterred from plunging so deep into legal strife by the fact that the defeated party becomes the slave of the successful one; so that, when a man has a case to be tried in this court, he risks not only the amount claimed in the original case, but the personal liberty of himself and family as well.

The case we saw decided was one in which, among other things, the ownership of about fifty slaves was involved.

The hour fixed was 10 A. M.; so we wended our way to the place of conflict. It was evidently a gala-day, and every spot of vantage-ground was occupied by interested spectators, — yes, interested in more senses than one; many of them having a good deal of money at stake in bets on the issue.

The old chief came down; but seeing the crowd I presume he thought there were plenty to see fair play, so he went back home. But royalty was still represented abundantly; and the wife, sons, daughter, and son-in-law of the old man remained to witness the trial.

The second chief was also there, as well as some Siamese officials, who have charge of all international business of the Zimmay Province.

Seats were given us among the grandees; and as we sat under the protection of a royal guard, we felt quite safe.

Scarcely are we seated before the litigants make their appearance, and take their places upon two bamboo platforms prepared for them. Each one is dressed in white, and surrounded by a number of friends and helpers. Each platform is surrounded by a lot of lighted candles; an offering of flowers is

A MARRIAGE CEREMONY IN JAVA.

made to the spirits who are supposed to preside over the water, which they are now about to enter.

They now proceed to prayers, in which they invoke the aid of the river-god and all good spirits, and call down upon themselves most frightful imprecations if their claim is unjust, or if they are attempting to deceive in any particular.

Two posts have been driven into the bottom of the river, in about three feet and a half or four feet of water.

The prayers being over, having a crown of wicker-work interwoven with flowers upon his head, and a rope tied around his waist, each principal is led down into the water by a single attendant.

Each one goes to his post and grasps it firmly in his hands, so that he may not be carried away by the swiftly flowing current. A long bamboo is now put from the shoulder of the one to the shoulder of the other.

And now comes the contest: they are to go under the water exactly the same moment, and the one who stays under the longer wins the case. Of course the supposition is that he has been helped by the spirits.

A hush goes over the vast assembly. The signal is given, and down, down they go slowly, — shoulders, chin, mouth, eyes, head, — all have disappeared; they are invisible, and the water flows over them without a ripple. The contestants are generally in such a terrible state of excitement that it is impossible for them to stay under long, a half-minute sometimes deciding the case.

But half a minute goes by, no sign from below; a minute, still invisible. Meanwhile the excitement on shore is intense.

A minute and a half; every breath is hushed, and every eye is fixed on those two posts in painful expectancy.

Two minutes is reached; not a voice is heard, although it is evident that it is only by a mighty effort the crowd is restrained.

At two minutes five seconds a head appears at the post nearest to the shore, and we see at once there is something wrong. The man has remained below until he has lost consciousness, and is being carried away by the current. Seeing this, his attendant catches him up and raises his head above water, and he has lost his case.

The case is decided; the pent-up emotion finds vent in yells, screams; and all is confusion.

Meanwhile, the friends of each man rush out to meet him; but how different the feelings animating each party! The one is carried in almost dead, and hurried out of the way; while the other was borne upon the shoulders of his friends in triumph, while others go before him singing, dancing, and showing their joy in all manner of impossible capers.

I could but feel sorry for the defeated one; for he had made a gallant fight, sticking to his post until he became insensible, and then of course he was brought to the surface solely in obedience to the laws of specific gravity.

But the spirits had decided; the case was settled. The son-in-law of the chief is in great spirits, having won four hundred rupees; while the second chief is very much dissatisfied: he lost seven hundred rupees; so he declares it was unfair, because the victor went under the water a second or so later than his opponent.

So ends the spectacle; but not so my thoughts upon the subject. It seems to me I have been away back into mediæval times, and witnessed a chapter from the history of our forefathers in the Middle Ages.

It is an experience I would not have missed for a great deal; and whenever in the future I read of a trial by combat, whether in history or fiction, I shall always have a vivid remembrance of what I saw on the banks of the Ma-Ping River in Northern Siam.

CHAPTER XVI.

THE FATE OF THE SEVEN MERCHANTS WHO BELIEVED LIES.

ALMOST every nation of the Orient has some story similar to the one we are about to tell. It is known among the Siamese and Burmese as the Story of Saw Kay. It is really a Karen story. We copy this version from a book called "The Loyal Karens of Burmah," by Donald M. Smeaton, of the Bengal Civil Service.

There once lived a great Karen called the Yellow Chief. He had a son named Saw Kay (Mr. Crooked). He was a cunning, idle, lazy fellow. The Burmese Government seized on the entire clan, and sent them under guard to cut a huge teak-tree into a war-boat and drag it to the river-bank. Saw Kay was the only male not seized. He was spared to carry the rice the women were forced to clean for the food of the working party. Saw Kay's mother had two large and very fat hogs, which she had petted so long that she could not bear to have them killed. Saw Kay's mouth watered every time he looked at their fat sides; and as his entreaties to be allowed to kill the hogs were in vain, he laid a plan to induce his mother to gratify his appetite for pork.

He went to his father, and with a profuse gush of tears told him that his mother was dead; sobbed out a pitiful tale of how his mother had been seized by cholera, and had died alone, deserted by all the women of the clan, and how he alone had buried the body and performed the funeral rites. Leaving his father under guard, plunged in the depth of woe at this untimely bereavement, he returned to his home and told his mother that his father, while at his work, had been killed by the boat rolling over on him. He described the fearful appearance of the corpse, mangled by the crushing weight that had mutilated it beyond recognition, and, beating on his breast, exclaimed against the brutality of the Burman guard that would not even permit the removal of the corpse to the ancestral burial-place (a terrible thing to Karens).

It must be remembered that Saw Kay was the only means of communication between the working party and their home, and that his lies ran no risk of detection.

The mother, bathed in tears, said, "Well, he was a good husband to me, and the least I can do will be to make the usual funeral feast to his memory, even if his bones do not lie with those of his fathers."

So one of the hogs was killed, and Saw Kay gorged himself to repletion. Soon after he began his plans for a second feast, and went to his father with proposals for a re-marriage. He said, "Father, we shall need some one to cook for us and weave our clothes. Now, I lately saw a woman who looked exactly like mother, — talked like her, and acted like her. In fact, if I had not buried mother with my own hands, I should have claimed her as my own mother. Now, you had better marry her. Let me act as the go-between and negotiate a marriage."

The father replied, "If she is like your dead mother, it is all I can ask;" and consented to the match.

Saw Kay then went to his mother, and told her that as soon as the clan returned from their work they would be driven from the long house in which the entire clan lived, in accordance with the ancestral Karen custom, which banished widows and orphans from the house, lest their misfortune prove contagious. He urged her to a second marriage, saying that he had met a man in the forest so strikingly resembling his father, that if he had not buried his father with his own hands, he should say it was his own father.

The mother said that if the proposed individual was only half as good as her deceased husband, it was enough, and consented to the match.

In this way Saw Kay was the first one to arrange a marriage between his own parents.

When the clan returned on the completion of the boat, the second hog was killed for the marriage feast.

Saw Kay, of course, presided, trusting to the impossibility of his parents having any private conversation in the crowd of invited guests. Both, of course, were much struck by the very peculiar resemblance to the supposed dead partner, but they had been prepared for this by Saw Kay's previous description. In high feather, Saw Kay performed the marriage ceremony over his parents, and ushered them to the bridal chamber.

Judging rightfully that "the ground would be too hot for him to tread on,"

ON A BAMBOO RAFT.

on the morrow, Saw Kay shouldered a hind-quarter of the hog slain for the feast, and marched to the "tai" (long mountain-house) of a neighboring clan.

He took care to time his arrival so as to find none of the men at home. When he entered the "tai," the women crowded around him, their mouths watering at the sight of the very fat hind-quarter of pork Saw Kay had brought with him. He reported that he had speared a wild hog too heavy to be carried home, and that he was returning for help to bring in the rest of the carcass.

"If you have a whole carcass, sell us this," spoke up an old woman; and she asked the price.

Saw Kay asked one hundred rupees for it. Karens then buried all their money for fear of the Burmese Government; and the woman, never seeing money, knew nothing of its value.

"Oh, if my husband were only at home, I'd make him buy me this delicious pork!" groaned the old woman.

"Go and ask him," said Saw Kay; "he is just beyond those bushes across the ravine."

The old woman ran round the head of the ravine, while Saw Kay whipped across unknown to her. On reaching the bushes, she shouted, "Husband, husband! may I buy a quarter of very fat pork for a hundred rupees?"

Saw Kay, from the other side of the bushes, called out, personating her husband, "Yes; and buy it quickly, lest you lose so good a bargain."

The old woman ran round, while Saw Kay rushed across the ravine, and was found sitting quietly in his place as if he had never stirred. The old woman dug up the money, and Saw Kay hastily left with his ill-gotten gains, rightly judging that the place would be too hot for him when the men returned from their work.

He then went down to the "Prince's Road," knowing that seven great Burmese merchants, with five hundred carts laden with up-country silk "patsoes," were soon to pass the spot. He carved a staff with peculiar figures on it, and buried his hundred rupees a few inches under the ground in little deposits of from two to five rupees each.

When his quick eye detected the merchants riding in advance of their carts, he pretended to be absorbed in his pursuits, and flourishing his staff with mystic passes he would shout, "Hey for five rupees!" strike the earth, and dig up the money.

The merchants watched the proceedings, saying to themselves, "Fool, not to wish for a lakh of rupees at once!"

On their approach Saw Kay feigned great fright, and tried to escape. The merchants held him fast, and tried to frighten him into a bargain for the magic staff. He pleaded hard to be allowed to keep it and said, "Perhaps the stick may be destined by fate for me alone."

The merchants threatened and offered money, until at last he, with apparent reluctance, sold the staff for a thousand rupees. The merchants dared not try their staff till they reached Rangoon, lest the possession of so great a treasure might cause them to be murdered by their own camp-followers. Of course the magic staff failed them. They were unable to search for Saw Kay till all their cargo of silk "patsoes" was disposed of, which took all the rainy season.

In the forest Saw Kay met a widow who had been driven from her clan and who had a posthumous daughter. Being brought up alone in a forest, the young girl had never seen a man. The tale waxes eloquent in praises of the young woman's beauty, and tells how the magic glance of her melting eye brought a body-guard of the most savage beasts around her; how whenever she stepped out into the sunshine the birds would close their ranks, flying over her so as to form a canopy over her to prevent her beautiful complexion from being tanned by the sun; how the carols of the birds accompanied her steps while walking; and how the birds watched in deathlike stillness over her siestas. It was a case of love at first sight, and the happy couple entered the nuptial state amid the wild enthusiasm of the beasts of the forest enslaved by the marvellous beauty of the lovely bride. The newly married couple spent the rainy season in the seclusion of the forest.

With the opening of the dry weather, the merchants came in great wrath to hunt down the dog of a Karen who had dared to cheat royal Burmese merchants.

With hundreds of their camp-followers they beat every strip of jungle and scoured every plain, till at last one morning Saw Kay's little hut was surrounded by men eagerly thirsting for his blood.

Hastily giving his wife and mother-in-law directions what to do, he sprang out on the veranda and seized a small bow hung there merely to frighten the crows, and commenced a wild dance with the most extravagant gestures to divert the attention of the men, closing up around him, from the attempt to escape of his wife and her mother. The two women stole away unperceived, as no one knew of Saw Kay's marriage and they were only on the look-out for the audacious Karen.

"Slave of a Karen!" shouted the merchants, as they seized on Saw Kay, "even your blood will not fully avenge the insult you have inflicted on us."

Saw Kay reminded them of the extreme reluctance with which he had parted with the magic staff, and of the threats by which his consent to the sale had been extorted, and told them the staff was evidently assigned by fate to him, and that they, unworthy on account of their avarice in grasping so much

RAFTING TEAK-WOOD.

at once, were unable to avail themselves of it. He pleaded to ears deafened by long-nursed rage. He then rose with dignity, and said: "Since nothing but blood will appease your anger, I refuse not to die. I only ask to be allowed before my death to give you all a good meal of fowl-curry, that I may die in the odor of sanctity, doing good even to my murderers."

"Dog of a Karen!" yelled his foes, "do not think to appease us by so trifling a gift."

"I hope not to soften your hard hearts; I only ask to depart this life in a forgiving spirit."

All the party were very hungry, and finally consented. Surrounded by guards holding ropes attached to his waist, and ordered to cut him down at the first attempt to escape, Saw Kay took the little bow and started with the whole party for the jungle, to shoot wild fowl for the curry he had promised. When wild fowl were met he refused to shoot, saying there were not enough in the flock to feed so many. He was really only making time for his wife and her mother to follow out his directions.

At last a large flock of wild fowl was met with, and he fired towards them; but the weak bow failed even to reach the fowls as they whirred away.

Saw Kay shouted after them, "Go home and cook yourselves! go home and cook yourselves!" and carefully concealed the bow while his captors were watching the fowls.

The merchants expressed their disgust at being thus fooled, and were on the point of killing him at once, but Saw Kay begged them to return to the hut and watch the result of his shot.

They did so, and found, to their surprise, a great pot of rice and a steaming kettle of capital fowl-curry that the two women had cooked, in the absence of the party, by Saw Kay's orders. While they enjoyed the feast the merchants said: "The scamp did certainly cheat us about the staff, but this bow is worth having. It would be very handy on our long journeys to have a bow which would not only shoot but cook our game for us." They offered Saw Kay his life if he would only give up the bow to them.

He refused, saying he was too lazy to work; and as his money was lost with the magic staff, and if now he lost his food with the magic bow, life was worthless to him.

To cut a long story short, they offered more and more, till finally they paid him a thousand rupees for the magic bow. Saw Kay, on his release, pushed with his wife and her mother still farther into the depths of the forest. Of course the magic bow failed as the magic staff had done.

With redoubled rage the Burmese merchants started afresh in search of the daring Karen who had twice outwitted them. After many days' fruitless search, they again surrounded Saw Kay's new hut.

The wife and mother attempted to escape again as before, but failed. Saw Kay concealed his wife in the house, and kept his mother-in-law with him on the veranda. As soon as his enemies came within hearing, Saw Kay said in a violent tone to his mother-in-law: "You wretched old wife of mine, how can any one live with a withered old crone like you? Become a virgin, or I will beat you with this rice-pestle till you do so."

He seized the old lady by the waist and threw her down violently and rolled her up in a mat, whispering to her to crawl out of the end of the mat and escape. The old woman this time succeeded, as the attention of every one was taken by the peculiar talk and gestures of their prey.

Saw Kay struck the roll of matting several very heavy blows with the rice pestle, shouting, "Become a virgin! become a virgin!" He threw the roll of matting across his shoulder and ran into the house.

His foes rushed into the house to seize him, but at the mere sight of the young and lovely wife all fell prostrate before her. They slowly arose, and with dazzled eyes bound their victim and took him to their masters, telling them they had with their own eyes seen a wrinkled, toothless old woman changed by the blows of the club into this lovely vision of beauty.

The merchants held a long consultation over the beauteous prize. They said: "We have been terribly cheated twice, it is true, but we see here that there can be no deception in this wonderful club. Our wives we married while young, and we love them too much to divorce them; yet we cannot but confess they are not as handsome as they once were. This club, renewing the youth and beauty of our wives, will be our most valuable possession."

After a long mixture of threats and tempting offers, the merchants bought the club for a thousand rupees, and returned to their camp on the plains, and the same evening all made widowers of themselves. The magic club, seemed as much a failure as the magic staff and the magic bow had been. The unfortunate wives, when taken out of the rolls of matting, were stone dead, killed by the blows they had received.

The merchants were, of course, wild with rage at being deceived the third time. Distrusting their own ability to cope with the wily Karen alone, they laid a formal complaint before the governor of the district, stationed at Myountaga, and begged that condign punishment might be meted out to the slave of a Karen who had dared repeatedly to cheat royal Burmese merchants.

A levy of every male between fourteen and sixty years of age was at once ordered, and the entire forest was carefully scoured.

A VILLAGE IN THE UPPER LAOS.

Hearing of Saw Kay's wonderful cunning, the governor ordered every one of the beaters ears to be carefully stopped with wax. Saw Kay was captured.

What were his pleas and how he tried to escape his fate, is unknown; as, owing to the governor's precaution, no one could hear a word he said.

Saw Kay was sentenced to death, and every Karen in the district was brought in to attend the execution, that hereafter no "dog of a Karen" should ever dare to take such liberties with their masters.

That each of the seven merchants might have a share in his death, Saw Kay was put into a long cylindrical basket with stones at each end to sink it, and the basket was laid on the brink of a steep bank which overhangs a deep pool in the river. At the word of command each merchant was to give a kick to the basket, and thus roll it into the river.

A grand breakfast was given by the merchants to all the assembled crowds in honor of the final victory over their cunning foe, which they now felt was secure. During breakfast Saw Kay was left alone in his basket, his guards deeming him securely fastened. They feared lest, in the scramble for breakfast, they might lose their share.

While everybody was away, an up-country boatman, with a cargo of silk "patsoes" and much jewelry, was attracted by the sight of the crowd, and thinking it might be a capital chance to sell his wares, he landed just where Saw Kay's basket lay.

"Hi! you fellow in the basket," he asked, "what are you doing there?"

Saw Kay replied: "The king at Ava is dead, and the astrologers have pronounced that I am the only one who can succeed him. I refused the crown; and as the astrologers have decided that in my lifetime no one else can peaceably ascend the throne, I am now to be drowned."

"Fool!" replied the boatman, "to avoid what any one would risk his life for, you give up your life."

Saw Kay piously talked of the many temptations of a kingly life, and the many deaths a king must cause, and said he had deliberately weighed temporal against eternal riches, and had chosen death rather than the throne.

"Ah!" said the boatman, "don't I wish I had your chance?"

"What will you give for it?" said Saw Kay.

"My boat and its cargo," replied the boatman.

"Agreed," was Saw Kay's reply. "Hurry and take my place before any one comes to notice our proceedings."

The boatman set the Karen at liberty, took his place, and was firmly tied in by Saw Kay, who quietly took his seat in his new boat to watch the execution.

When breakfast was over, the drums beat to assemble the crowds, the bands began to play, and the dancers to celebrate the victory of the royal Burman over the despised Karen. As the merchants advanced to roll their enemy into the river, the poor boatman shouted from the basket with all his might, "I *will* be king! I *will* be king!"

"A great *king* you'll be!" was the reply, as the merchants rolled him into the pool. The rest of the day was spent in feasting and dancing to celebrate the victory over the Karens. Next morning, as the merchants were packing their carts for their return, Saw Kay walked into the camp with sublime impudence, with jewelry all over his person and silk "patsoes" hanging over his arms and shoulders, the spoils of the up-country boatman.

Every jaw fell, and stammeringly they asked him how he came there.

"Didn't I say yesterday that I would be a king? Now I am one. It happened that the road to heaven leads right into that pool, and you rolled me exactly into the road that leads to the abodes of the blest. There I saw all your deceased relatives and ancestors, who expressed great wonder that none of you ever visited them. They have sent you these gifts to show you the marvellous riches of that glorious country. I could not bear to return, but your friends begged me so hard to return and show you the way, that I could not refuse."

"How can we go?" asked the merchants.

"Easily," replied Saw Kay. "Make me eight baskets, and I will tie you into seven of them and follow you in the eighth."

The baskets were made. Saw Kay rolled the merchants into the pool, and returned with all their wealth to Mya-yah-doung.

JUDGE HARE AND HIS WONDERFUL DECISIONS.

In the following stories Judge Hare is made to act the part somewhat like that assigned to "Brother Rabbit" in the negro cabins of the South.

A tiger and a hare once made a friendship by drinking together the mingled blood of both (a Karen custom to this day). The tigers then were pure yellow without stripes. They went off to cut thatch for their houses.

The tiger took his breakfast done up in a parcel. The hare made up a bundle of offal to resemble the tiger's breakfast parcel. Both cut busily away at the thatch till breakfast-time, when the hare went to the tree under which their parcels had been placed, and called the tiger to breakfast.

THE CITY OF XIENG MAÏ, IN THE UPPER LAOS

The tiger said he could not come just then, for he wanted to cut more thatch before the sun became too hot to work.

The hare replied, "Don't you know that when you are late to breakfast your food changes to offal?"

The tiger went on cutting thatch, and the hare ate up all his breakfast.

When the sun became hot, the tiger came in hungry, and found nothing but offal in what he took for his own parcel. "Did n't I tell you so?" said the hare.

Soon the hare pretended to have a severe attack of fever, and the tiger offered to carry him home.

"How can I ever stick on your smooth glossy back?" said the hare. "You must tie some bundles of thatch on your back to form a saddle for me."

The tiger firmly bound some bundles of dry thatch on his back, and the hare crawled upon them. On their way home the hare began striking his flint and steel together.

"What noise is that?" asked the tiger.

"Only my teeth chattering with the ague," replied the hare.

Soon the hare blew the sparks into a blaze, and jumped off, laughing at the fearful scorching borne by the unfortunate tiger, who bears the marks of his burns to-day in his stripes.

The tiger, of course, set off in pursuit of the hare.

The hare, seeing him coming, climbed up into a bee-tree, and crawled up to the bees so stealthily as not to be noticed by them.

The tiger roared out, "Come down and I'll swallow you alive, you faithless friend."

"There are white, black, gray, and speckled hares; I'm not the only hare," replied he. "Prove that I am guilty before you eat me."

The tiger could not do so, and, accepting the denial of the hare, asked him what he was doing there.

"I am watching my grandfather's fan," was the reply.

"What's your grandfather's fan good for?" asked the tiger.

"Oh, it cools you off without the trouble of fanning yourself. Can't you hear the rushing of the wind from it?" was the reply.

The tiger mistook the murmur of the bees for the breeze, and, smarting with his terrible burns, thought that a self-acting punkah would be very handy just then, and so asked to be allowed to watch "his grandfather's fan" for the hare for a few hours, — for you must know bees build in a semi-circular, fanlike shape under a bough in Burmah.

The hare consented, and told the tiger that a gentle pat with his paw would increase the current of air to any desired extent. The tiger crawled up, and lay at full length on the limb; but, feeling no cooling breeze, struck the bees with his paw. Of course he was attacked by the whole swarm, and nearly killed by their stings. With redoubled rage the tiger started again in pursuit.

The hare awaited his arrival where two trees crossed their trunks and creaked with every gust of wind.

"Come here, you doubly faithless friend, and I'll swallow you alive," roared the tiger.

As before, the hare pleaded an alibi, and challenged the tiger to prove his identity with the hare that had wronged him. The tiger, with no proof at hand, accepted the hare's statement, and asked him what he was doing there.

"Oh, I'm watching over my grandfather's harp," was the reply. "Can't you hear its song?"

"What's the good of your grandfather's harp?" asked the tiger.

"Oh, it lulls you to sleep in spite of all pain," answered the wily hare.

The tiger, smarting with his burns and the stings of the bees, longed to forget his pain in sleep, and so asked to be allowed to take the hare's place for a few hours. The hare consented, and told the tiger he had only to put his paw between the trees when the wind blew, and the most enchanting airs of music would soon waft him to dreamland. Of course, the tiger's paw was caught between the trees and fearfully crushed.

Thrice cheated, the tiger again limped off in pursuit. This time he found the hare had fallen into a pit dug to catch game. When called on to surrender himself for death, the hare denied his identity as before, and said, —

"How could I have cheated you so when I have been watching my grandfather's game-pit all the time? Here I have more game than I can eat."

The tiger, smarting with burns and stings and crippled in one paw, could no longer run down game, and so asked permission to jump down into the pit and eat the game that fell in.

The hare agreed, and, as soon as the tiger was safe in the pit, began tickling his burns with a straw.

"Stop that or I'll throw you out of the pit," said the tiger.

The hare kept on tickling, and at last the tiger threw him out of the pit altogether. The hare then ran to some Shans, who had dug the pit, and told them that a tiger had fallen into a pit, and the Shans killed the tiger.

The hare, from his great wisdom, soon became the umpire to whose decision all the disputes of the forest were referred. Among many famous decisions of his is that of the case of the tiger and the boar.

"HE SEIZED THE MAN AND WAS ABOUT TO DEVOUR HIM."

THE TIGER AND THE BOAR.

A tiger and a wild boar were brought up as foster-brethren, and pledged themselves to an eternal friendship. The boar became very fat as he reached maturity, and the tiger's mouth watered every time he looked at his friend's fat sides, and he began to seek an excuse for eating him.

One morning the tiger went, with much feigned sadness, to the boar, and told him he had been disturbed by bad dreams, saying, "I dreamed that I ate you, and your fat sides tasted deliciously."

"Well, what of that?" said the boar.

"The trouble is," replied the tiger, "we tigers have an ancestral custom which compels us to make true any dream we have; and so, however reluctant to break our friendship, I *must* eat you."

The boar refused to be bound by any tiger's custom, and after great dispute they agreed to defer the matter to the nearest King, and set out for his court. When they reached the palace, the tiger told the boar to go right in, and he would follow soon. The boar took his seat in the audience chamber; but the tiger secured a private meeting with the King, and offered him a bribe of a hind quarter of the boar to decide in his favor.

Crowds assembled to witness the strange spectacle of a lawsuit between two wild animals. The sight of the boar's fat sides made the mouths of the King and Queen and nobles water till the floor was bedewed with saliva. The bribe, so tempting, of course caused the case to be prejudged. The tiger pleaded the sanctity of ancestral customs, and with plentiful tears bewailed his sad fate in being *compelled* to eat so valued a friend.

The boar pleaded the inviolability of the ties which bound them together. The boar pleaded in vain; for his fatness showed so temptingly the bribe the tiger had offered, that the case went against him. When the decision was made the boar demanded seven days in which to dispose of his property and make provision for his family, and was released, after taking a solemn oath to return for death on that day week. While sadly visiting his old haunts, the boar met the hare, and was asked why he looked so sorrowful. The boar replied by telling of the sad fate that awaited him.

"When? In such an insignificant case as this hire *me* as your lawyer," said the hare.

The boar, of course, retained the hare as his legal adviser, and on the appointed day the two went to court together.

The boar claimed the right to bring further pleas in his case, as he was now represented by proper legal counsel. The hare panted and pretended to be completely out of breath, and said he must have a nap to rest him before he could do full justice in so important a case. A mat was spread for him, and the hare pretended to drop asleep, while the King and Queen and nobility looked with watering mouths at the fat sides of the boar.

At last the hare sprang up, and, clasping his hands in ecstasy, he exclaimed: "What a glorious dream I have had! I dreamed that I eloped with the Queen. We hares have an ancestral custom that we *must* make good every dream we have; so I *must* elope with the Queen."

With that he seized the Queen's hand, and began dragging her away.

The King saw he must reverse his previous decision in the case of tiger and boar; so he hastily decided against the sanctity of ancestral customs, and freed the boar.

THE TIGER AND THE MAN.

A poor "toungya" cultivator left his basket every morning in his hut in the "toungya," and a tiger came and stole it every day. The man, in his anger, set a trap of huge logs so arranged as to fall on any animal that touched the bait. The tiger was caught and badly crushed by the logs, but was still alive. When the man came in on hearing the roars, the tiger pleaded hard for his life. He admitted the daily theft, but urged that theft was not a capital crime, and that he had been so severely punished already by the fall of the trap that he ought in justice to be released from the trap.

The man refused, saying he feared the tiger would eat him if released. The tiger swore most solemnly never to attempt revenge, and was released.

As soon as he was out of the trap he seized the man and was about to devour him. The man pleaded the sanctity of the oath just taken. The tiger said necessity knew no law, and that, crippled as he was, he could no longer catch game for his daily food, but *must* eat the man or starve.

The hare happened to be passing, and the case was referred to him for decision.

The hare, with a wise look, said, "I can't understand this matter clearly. Now you both act out just what each did."

The man told where he hid his breakfast every day, and showed how he set the trap, and made the man set it to show how it was done. The tiger was then ordered to show what he did, and accordingly entered the trap, but walked round gingerly, carefully avoiding the spring of the trap.

"I don't see that anything happened to you that you can justly complain of," said the hare. "How could you have received these terrible bruises?"

"THE ELEPHANT BEGGED FOR A WEEK'S DELAY."

The tiger edged nearer and nearer, till at last he touched the spring and the trap fell again.

"Out *dah*[1] and attack him!" said the hare, "and never again restore an advantage to an enemy too strong for you."

THE TIGER AND THE ELEPHANT.

A tiger and an elephant once made a bet as to which was the larger. The winner was to eat the loser. They agreed to leave the decision to the men of a neighboring village. Both were to go near the village and roar by turns, and listen to what the villagers said. The elephant roared first. It is well known that the elephant never roars except when in pain; so the villagers said, "What ails that little elephant? What can be attacking him?" The tiger then roared, and the villagers said at once, "There! it's a tiger that is attacking the little elephant. He must be a monster to prey on elephants."

"There! do you hear that?" said the tiger. "You are pronounced a little elephant, while I am called a monster. Now I'll eat you."

The elephant begged for a week's delay to enable him again to visit his birthplace and his ancient feeding-grounds, and to bid good-by to his family. The respite was granted, and the elephant swore to be on hand at the appointed day.

The elephant, on revisiting the pool in which he was accustomed to drink, wept so profusely over his sad fate that his tears made the stream salt. The hare lived farther down the stream; and when he found his drinking-water brackish, he started up stream to see what had defiled the water.

When he found the elephant, he asked why he looked so thin in flesh, and why he wept so profusely. The elephant told the story of the lost bet; and the hare laughingly replied, "If that is all, hire me as your lawyer, and I'll soon set you free."

The hare's legal services were retained, and both proceeded together on the appointed day to the rendezvous. They went a little early.

The hare told the elephant to feign death, and when he bit him on the ear to raise his head, and when he pulled him by the end of the trunk to move in the direction in which he was pulled.

As soon as the tiger came near, he saw the hare skipping over the huge, apparently dead carcass, every now and then nibbling the ear of the elephant, when the huge head of the elephant would rise as if the hare had lifted it. Every now and then the hare would pull at the trunk, and the whole body of

---

[1] A long-handled knife or cleaver.

the elephant would roll over as if by the efforts of the hare. The tiger thought the hare had killed his elephant, and said to himself, "That's a wonderfully strong little fellow to kill my elephant and drag the body about so easily. I don't believe even I am a match for him. I'll try and get my elephant peaceably, but I shall not dare risk a fight with a beast that can kill and drag about a whole elephant like that." On going nearer, the tiger said, "Hallo! what are you doing with my elephant?"

The hare replied in a grumbling tone, as if his mouth were full of food, "One elephant is not enough for my breakfast; have you come to eke out my meal with your flesh?"

The tiger, in great fright, said, "I came to eat, and not to be eaten;" and rushed in terror to the dense jungle, roaring with rage at losing his food.

THE HARE AND THE KING.

A certain King once was so proud that he became almost unendurable to his subjects. The hare went to rebuke him.

He came into the court and called out, "Hey, you fellow! who are you, anyway?"

The answer was, "I am the King."

The hare replied, "Well, I am only a jungle beast, and don't know what 'king' means."

"A king is one who has nothing above him," was the reply.

"Well, I declare! Is there nothing above you?" questioned the hare, with a look of astonishment.

"Nothing," answered the King.

"Well, I never saw a man with nothing above him before, and I want to take a good look at you."

"Look your fill!" the King replied.

The hare stared at the King for hours, till an urgent call of hunger led the King to attempt to leave the Court quietly, without attracting notice. The hare called out, "Hey, you King! where are you going to?"

The King, abashed, sat down again.

This was repeated several times, till the King could hold out no longer, and blurted out, "If you must know, I'm hungry."

"Ah, you're no king!" shouted the hare; "your own bowels are your master. They demand food, and you are powerless to resist." The hare then went on to show him death, sickness, and old age were all above him, and that he must obey them, and that by his own definition only God was king.

CHAPTER XVII.

THE CREMATION OF A KING.

HOW greatly the missionary was needed in Siam might be easily illustrated by the manner in which sickness is treated, and in the cruel ceremonies that attend the birth of children and the funeral rites. Bowring gives a prescription used in fevers, which must have been the product of a genius of superstition. It was as follows: —

"One portion of rhinoceros horn, one of elephant's tusk, one of tiger's, and the same of crocodile's teeth; one bear's tooth, one portion composed of three parts bones of vulture, raven, and goose; one portion of bison, and another of stag's horn, one portion of sandal."

Bowring says: —

"When a Siamese is dying, the priests are sent for, who recite passages which speak of the vanity of earthly things from their sacred books, and cry out, repeating the exclamation in the ears of the dying, —

"'Arahang! arahang!' (a mystical word implying the purity of Buddha.)

"When the dying has heaved his last breath, the whole family utter piercing cries, and address their lamentations to the departed: —

"'O father benefactor! why leave us? What have we done to offend you? Why depart alone? It was your own fault. Why did you eat the fruit that caused the dysentery? We foretold it; why did not you listen to us? Oh, misery! Oh, desolation! Oh, inconstancy of human affairs!'

"They fling themselves at the feet of the dead, weep, wail, kiss, utter a thousand tender reproaches, till grief has exhausted its lamentable expressions.

"The body is then washed and enveloped in white cloth; it is placed in a coffin covered with gilded paper, and decorated with tinsel flowers; a daïs is prepared, ornamented with the same materials as the coffin, but with wreaths of flowers and a number of wax-lights.

"After a day or two the coffin is removed, not through the door, but through an opening specially made in the wall; the coffin is escorted thrice round the house at full speed, in order that the dead, forgetting the way through which he has passed, may not return to molest the living.

"The coffin is then taken to a large barge and placed on a platform, surmounted by the daïs, to the sound of melancholy music. The relations and friends, in small boats, accompany the barge to the temple where the body is to be burnt. Being arrived, the coffin is opened and delivered to the officials charged with the cremation, the corpse having in his mouth a silver tical (2s. 6d. in value) to defray the expenses. The burner first washes the face of the corpse with cocoa-nut milk; and if the deceased have ordered that his body shall be delivered to vultures and crows, the functionary cuts it up and distributes it to the birds of prey which are always assembled in such localities. The corpse being placed upon the pile, the fire is kindled. When the combustion is over, the relatives assemble, collect the principal bones, which they place in an urn, and convey them to the family abode. The garb of mourning is white, and is accompanied by the shaving of the head. The funerals of the opulent last for two or three days. There are fireworks, sermons from the bonzes, nocturnal theatricals, where all sorts of monsters are introduced. Seats are erected within the precincts of the temples, and games and gambling accompany the rites connected with the dead."

The cremation of a dead king is a great national event in Siam. No coronation could be more imposing. The solemnity of death adds to the dramatic effect of the rituals. Kings from Laos, and princes from afar add to the splendor of the last awful rites.

The cremation ceremonies of 1870 were of this spectacular character. The temple of the pyre was starred with gold. Says an eyewitness, —

"Below, the temple had four entrances leading directly to the pyre; upon each side, as you entered, were placed magnificent mirrors, which reflected the whole interior of the building, which was decorated with blue and gold, in the

A BREAK-NECK RIDE.

same manner as the exterior. From the roof depended immense chandeliers, which at night increased the effect beyond description. Sixteen large columns, running from north to south, supported the roof. The entire height of the building must have been one hundred and twenty feet, its length about fifty feet, and breadth forty feet. In the centre was a raised platform, about seven feet high, which was the place upon which the urn containing the body was to be placed; upon each side of this were stairs covered with scarlet and gold cloth.

"Upon the first day of the ceremonies, when I rose at daylight, I was quite surprised at the number and elegance of the large boats that were dashing about the river in every direction; some of them with elegantly formed little spires (two in each boat) of a snowy-white, picked out with gold; others with magnificent scarlet canopies, with curtains of gold; others filled with soldiers dressed in red, blue, or green, according to their respective regiments; the whole making a most effective tableau, far superior to any we had during the time the embassy was here.

"Whilst I was admiring this scene, I heard the cry of 'Sedet' (the name of the King when he goes out), and turning round, beheld the fleet of the King's boats sweeping down. His Majesty stopped at the 'men,' where an apartment had been provided for him. The moment the King left his boat, the most intense stillness prevailed,—a silence that was absolutely painful; this was, after the lapse of a few seconds, broken by a slight stroke of a tom-tom. At that sound every one on shore and in the boats fell on their knees, and silently and imperceptibly the barge containing the high-priest parted from the shore at the Somdetch's palace, and floated with the tide towards the 'men.'

"This barge was immediately followed by that containing the urn, which was placed upon a throne in the centre of the boat. One priest knelt upon the lower part of the urn in front, and one at the back. (It had been constantly watched since his death.) Nothing could exceed the silence and *immovability* of the spectators; the tales I used to read of nations being turned to statues were here realized, with the exception that all had the same attitude. It was splendid, but it was fearful. During the whole of the next day the urn stayed in the 'men,' in order that the people might come and pay their last respects.

"The urn, or rather its exterior cover, was composed of the finest gold, elegantly carved and studded with innumerable diamonds. It was about five feet high, and two feet in diameter.

"Upon the day of the burning, two Kings arrived about four P. M. The golden cover was taken off, and an interior urn of brass now contained the body, which rested upon cross-bars at the bottom of the urn. Beneath were all kinds of odoriferous gums.

"The first King, having distributed yellow cloths to an infinite number of priests, ascended the steps which led to the pyre, holding in his hand a lighted candle, and set fire to the inflammable materials beneath the body.

"The next day the bones were taken out of the urn, and given to the King's relatives."

The fireworks on the river on the nights of such cremation services are inconceivably splendid. The river runs fire, and the sky is flame.

There have been several influences on Siam during the last half-century, which have silently changed the thought and habits of the people. One of them is the introduction of modern inventions, and another is the missionary work among the Chinese population. But a very important influence on the late King and Court has been that of a woman. In writing and editing this medley of stories illustrating the Siamese peninsula, and what we may teach Siam, and what we may learn from it, and what it may teach us, we have made use of several of the stories of Mrs. Leonowens by her special permission. These stories were originally written for an American periodical, which permitted their use here. Mrs. Leonowens was, as we have stated, for a considerable time a governess in the Siamese Court, and her works, "Life in the Harem," and "An English Governess in a Siamese Court," are very well known to readers of the best literature of ten years ago, and would be excellent reading to follow this story. This lady's influence on the King and Court led to a great change of customs, and enlargement of liberal thought and policy of the government. In Siam the King is the kingdom, and whatever influences the King moulds the State.

The railroad-builders and linemen, of whom Mr. C. A. Stephens has written many delightful stories of adventure, have also been pioneers of a better and higher order of civilization. They have prepared, and are preparing, the field for the missionary. Says George B. Bacon, in "Siam:"—

"At first sight these years of missionary effort might seem to have resulted in failure. The statistics show but little accomplished; the roll of communicants seems insignificant. And of the sincerity and intelligence even of this small handful there are occasional misgivings. And on the whole, those who are quick to criticise and to oppose foreign missions might seem to have a good argument, and to find a case in point, in the history of missions in Siam.

"But really the success of these efforts has been extraordinary, although the history of them exhibits an order of results almost without precedent. Ordinarily, the religious enlightenment of a people comes first, and the civilization follows as a thing of course. But here the Christianization of the nation has scarcely begun, but its civilization has made (as this volume has abundantly shown) much more than a beginning.

"The medical missionaries, by their charitable work among the rich, in the healing of disease, and by instituting various sanitary and precautionary expedients, have done much to familiarize all classes with the excellence of Western science, and to draw attention and respect to the civilization which they represent. It is due to the Christian missionaries, and (without any disparagement to the excellence of the Roman Catholic priests) we may say especially to the American missionaries, more than to any enterprise of commerce or shrewdness of diplomacy, that Siam is so far advanced in its intercourse with other nations."

In this hard field the American missionaries are still patiently at work; and what Mr. Taylor says in his work on "Siam" is true to-day. There is a great influence exerted without *direct* results. The character of the people is slowly changing under the teaching of the Gospel and the advance of science; but the change has come like a change of seasons, almost unobserved.

CHAPTER XVIII.

IVORY'S DEATH.

ON Christmas day there came flying to Rangoon a courier with a dreadful message. The Decoits had raided the country and killed a great number of people.

I was anxious to hear from the surveying party. The courier had learned their safety, — all but one.

Who was he? The courier did not know.

"The Decoits were preparing to burn an old Burmese woman in her hut, and *he* died in defending her. *He* was shot down."

It could not have been Ivory. His spirit, so full of tenderness and sentiment, would not have been equal to an encounter like that.

Yet something told me that the young man was Ivory. The thought haunted me; it came to me in vivid dreams; in fact, it made life like a vivid dream.

Two days after Christmas the two linemen came to Rangoon. I saw them as they rode up to the hotel. My heart grew hot as I strained my eyes in vain for Ivory.

Their faces turned white as they caught my eye.

"Where is Ivory?" I asked with an unsteady voice.

"Have you not heard? Did not the courier tell you?"

"No — what?"

"We escaped."

IVORY'S TOMB AT BANGKOK.

"Yes."

"But he stayed behind to help a bedridden woman."

"Yes."

"And they shot him."

There was a silence.

"He might have escaped. But the woman begged him not to leave her. We urged him to come away, but he said, 'I cannot leave her.' We told him that he would be shot and—"

"What?"

"His only reply was, 'I do not fear death at all; I should be afraid not to do my duty. You may go, but I *must* defend the poor creature or die.' He left his coat in one of our houses. We have brought it to you."

I went to my room. I did not leave it for several days.

On New Year's day I examined the pockets of the coat with a trembling hand. I found only a handkerchief and a small blank book. In the book was a poem.

ALEXANDER WILSON'S LAST WISH.

In some wild forest shade,
Under some spreading oak, or waving pine,
Or old elm, festooned with the budding vine,
    Let me be laid.

In this dim lonely grot
No foot intrusive will disturb my dust,
But o'er me songs of the wild birds shall burst,
    Cheering the spot.

Not amid charnel stones,
Or coffins dark and thick with ancient mould,
With tattered pall and fringe of cankered gold,
    May rest my bones.

But let the dewy rose,
The snowdrop and the violet, lend perfume
Above the spot where, in my grassy tomb,
    I take repose.

> Year after year,
> Within the silver birch-tree o'er me hung,
> The chirping wren shall rear her callow young,
> Shall build her dwelling near.
>
> And at the purple dawn of day
> The lark shall chant a pealing song above,
> And the shrill quail shall pipe her song of love.
> When eve grows dim and gray.
>
> The blackbird and the thrush,
> The golden oriole, shall flit around,
> And waken with a mellow gust of sound
> The forest's solemn hush.
>
> Birds from the distant sea
> Shall sometimes hither flock on snowy wings,
> And soar above my dust in airy rings,
> Singing a dirge to me.

Who wrote these lines?

They were printed and evidently cut from some American paper.

I have read them a hundred times with tears.

I have never met any one like Ivory. There was a mystery in his life and in his death that I cannot solve. I can only say that no life with any noble purpose is lived in vain.

It was in this discursive way and through these strange circumstances that I came to see and live in the Antipodes. It is not often, I think, that a hotel clerk and telegrapher is called to pursue an active life in his early years on opposite sides of the world.

www.ingramcontent.com/pod-product-compliance
Lightning Source LLC
Chambersburg PA
CBHW030017240426
43672CB00007B/983